HEALING
45 Year Journey

Agnes McGuennis
4/5/18

FOREWORD

"Agnes, in this volume, has given us the benefit of her life of research, of healing, and of treating others. She certainly possesses a God-given gift which she has faithfully exercised in the service of all those who have called upon her for help with health problems over the course of a long lifetime.

The case histories speak for themselves and each one demonstrates a different aspect of Agnes's expertise. There seems to be no limit to her ability to diagnose and having ascertained the problem, no limit to her knowledge of the remedies required. Often these are natural remedies or simple procedures that effect complete cures, many times as the result of the simplest action. One is left amazed at the scope of her intuition.

Like the Gospel story of the talents, far from burying hers, Agnes has developed them for the benefit of the needy of the world, who have come to her in their thousands seeking help. She has not spared herself and now her expertise is documented for posterity in her book.

Sr M Lydwina Farrell CP
Vice President BTTI
(Bio-testing and Therapy International)

Disclaimer

The opinions provided and statements made herein are my own. They are not intended to diagnose, prevent or recommend any drug or natural remedy for any disease. You should obtain medical or professional advice for your personal requirements.

My special thanks to Emer Bourke and Orla Murphy who did the painstaking work of sifting through my files and papers to enable this volume to be put together. Our hope is that it will be of benefit to people for future health needs.

The case histories in Chapter 8 are written by the clients in their own words.

Contents:

Introduction

It has been a privilege for me to have been able to develop a second career for myself in natural healthcare. I had from a young age harboured the thoughts of being able to help people especially with their health issues. Nursing would have been an ambition, medicine would have been a dream. As life progressed neither happened, that's why I refer to a second career, which developed soon after my 40th birthday.

The details and opinions I express herein are clearly my own based on experiences in practice combined with published articles and books that emerged over the years. The opinions, advice and remedies are not intended to be a substitute for medical advice or conventional medical treatments. There is no intention herein to diagnose any condition or disease. Readers should always consult with their doctor or health professional.

I take this opportunity to thank the many people who helped me on this journey. Firstly, my late mother for the inspiration she was when I was a child. My gratitude goes to my late husband Paddy McGuinness who was encouraging and supportive of me throughout our life together. After practice got underway, my days became very busy as I saw approx. 30 clients per week for some 30 years scaling it back over the past ten years. I thank every one of you for your confidence in me and for your friendship. During an extremely busy period of practice my daughter in law, Lorna McGuinness joined to help out with the workload. However such was that workload that she stayed for 17 years as Administrator of the practice. I am grateful to Lorna for her time and energy for such a long period.

The practice of natural medicine changed considerably over my 45 years. In the early years training and support was sparse but it has expanded in diversity and content so I am grateful to all of those pioneers who shared their skills so willingly with the rest of the community. I am grateful to the many other practitioners who shared their knowledge and experiences so willingly so that the public could benefit. I refer to just a few of those wonderful people in Chapter 2. With chronic illness levels growing year by year demands on the health services are growing in tandem. I believe there is a compelling need for more choice and diversity in healthcare so incorporating natural therapies into mainstream healthcare is a sensible way forward. I encourage every individual who is interested in a career in natural therapy to believe in yourself, believe in your dream and go for it. It will be lifelong learning.

Love and good health to all.
Agnes

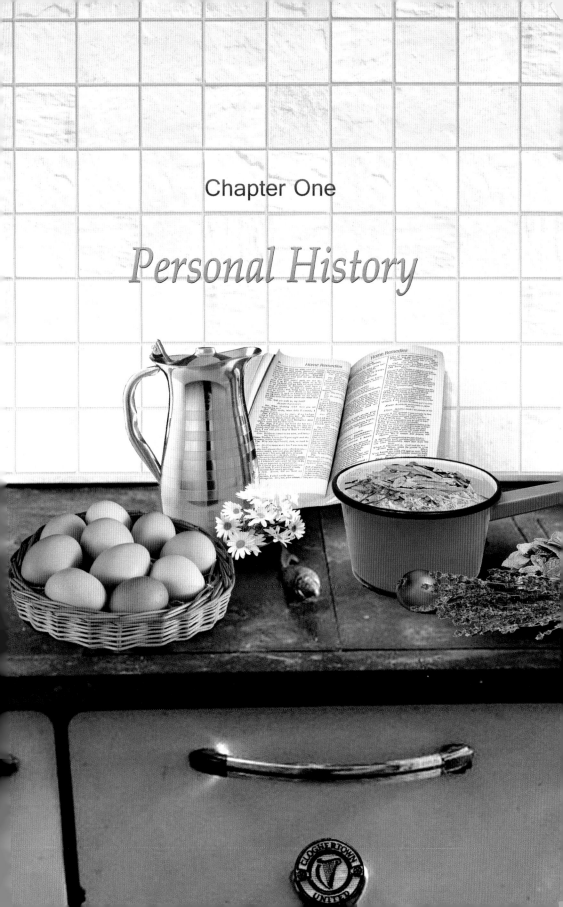

Chapter One

Personal History

Personal History

I was born on the 25th February, 1932 in Oldtown, Co. Dublin. It was a home birth as was customary at the time and I was the third child in a family of five. We had three boys and two girls in the family. My father was a few years older than my mother. My mother Margaret died at the age of 48 years from cancer. I recall her as a great homemaker. We had a little over one acre of land around the family home. On that, we had one cow to provide milk for the family. Oats was grown to feed the cow and provide straw for winter bedding. A small section was fenced off where two pigs were kept. They had a pen in which they could lie and sleep but lived and foraged outside for the most part. The apple garden was also fenced with net wire to keep the hens in and the fox out.
The hens foraged under the apple trees and had an enclosed roost for the night. The remainder was essentially a kitchen garden with a great variety of fruit, herbs and vegetables. At season end, Mam bottled all her fruits. Vegetables were seasonal. During winter, the rhubarb roots were covered with farmyard manure and the artichokes roots with straw. This procedure was to have fresh produce shortly after St Patricks day following.

By May we had fresh lettuce and cabbage, in June new potatoes and so on. Greens such as lettuce, spinach, scallions, cabbage and broccoli were summer regulars with onions, turnips and vegetable soups were frequent winter foods. Every April, a pig was taken to the slaughter house which was the barn of a nearby farmer. Four local families participated and each had their pig slaughtered in turn every two weeks. So over an eight week period we had fresh pork products, especially the inners and offal cuts. I have great memories of the fresh black pudding which as children we used to love to see boil in the pig pot. The next day there would be rings of them waiting for the pan. That process was repeated in the autumn and it was a great form of community sharing; everybody benefited. Unfortunately, it died out sometime in the sixties. Soon after slaughter, the sides of bacon were heavily salted and stored in wooden crates. There was then enough bacon available for six months. I didn't care too much for the salted bacon, but bacon, cabbage and potatoes had been the staple diet of the Irish people for hundreds of years. Saturday was the fixed day for bacon and cabbage in our house. Sunday, it was chicken from the home plot. Every few weeks we had beef from the butchers. In my earlier years as a child, I recall that both the chicken and beef were boiled. With the arrival of electric cookers and the range in the kitchen, roasting replaced boiling. With that we lost some nutrients as the chicken carcass would be used again to make soup or stocks. Potatoes were standard at dinner-time every day. All baking was with wholemeal flour. Niceties included apple tart served with custard after Sunday dinner. During the summer months, it would be rhubarb tart and custard.

Scones covered with homemade jam were a regular treat. Breakfast was always simple, porridge most days with a boiled egg and brown bread on other days. For my parents, and as the children got older, some mornings it would be fried rashers and eggs for breakfast in winter time, with fresh scallions replacing the eggs in summertime.

I recall Mam boiling up Senna leaves every Saturday and all of us had to drink this infusion and were told it would keep us free from intestinal parasites. She added laurel leaves to milk which she boiled and strained then made rice pudding with milk as a mineral rich desert. She also made white sauce from milk and laurel leaf which she would pour over the bacon and the cauliflower.

A vivid recollection I have is the recycling and reuse. Mam would wash the flour bags and cut them into strips as bandages for people who would call with sores on their feet. She would rub salted butter onto the bandages to disinfect the sores. The used flour bags would routinely be used for making shirts, pillowcases and sheets. All edible kitchen waste went to feed the hens and the pigs as did garden waste such as carrot and parsnip leaves and unused roots.

Death of my Mother

It was a terrible tragedy for us when Mam died of cancer - she was 48. I was 11 years old at that stage. Thankfully the time of her diagnosis to her death was quite short so she didn't have to suffer. Despite her short lifespan, she had influenced us greatly and served the family with generosity and love. My father had been diagnosed with cancer of the face some years earlier. He was treated in Dublin and had surgery to remove one side of his jaw including the bone.
He was in hospital for a long period and I recall every week Mam took us on the bus to Dublin. She was only able to take one of the children, occasionally two, to visit him. I recall those trips to Dublin very well.

I think Mam was a big influence in encouraging the hospital to discharge Dad, believing that he would be better off at home, and living in the environment that he knew. I was present on the day when I heard the polite conversation as she encouraged the doctor to discharge him. It was some decades later that I fully understood the importance of bringing him home, the nurturing and nursing he received. He was an outdoors man, he recovered his strength.
He got back into the home diet which included special soups, mashed cauliflower, minced meat and mashed potato, all of which had a sprinkling of parsley and other herbs. He started to do outdoor jobs particularly gardening as before. He regained his strength and his enjoyment of life and lived to the age of 78 years.

Soon after Mam's death, there was change in the family. My elder siblings were at secondary school so it would not have been practical to disrupt their education. My two younger siblings were too young to leave home. As the middle child, I was the one, and in hindsight I believe it was the correct choice by Dad, that I go and live with a relative. I went to live with my mother's aunt Jeanie McGrath, who lived in Clonalvy in Co Meath. Jeanie was the postmistress in Clonalvy, she had never married and she lived alone. She was great to me, she was like a mother. I got on well in my new school, had a few new pals in a short time. Nevertheless, I missed the companionship, the rivalry and competition of family life. It was now so much quieter with just my great aunt and myself in the house. I would recall my earlier years of childhood especially the Saturday evening washtub and scrub-up, polishing of shoes and preparation of clothes for mass. Sunday was an important day and mass attendance was compulsory in our household. The outfit was described as your Sunday best, it was a mark of respect for the Mass and the Church. We had the family rosary every evening when we all knelt down together to pray. It was a daily routine for us as it was in every other household. Faith, mass, prayer and the love of God has remained with me and has always been a powerful influence in my life. I felt God was with me every day.

I missed home at Christmas especially the first Christmas in Clonalvy. The making of the Christmas pudding in late November and the making of Christmas cakes were all memories. Finding a Christmas Tree, decorating it, blowing of balloons, collection of stickers and so on. Then it was preparation for Santa and all the excitement. My younger siblings were still at the Santa age at the time I left home so it was still fresh in my mind. Christmas at the Post Office was altogether different. It was a busy period both the PO and the shop. People wanted to send telegrams, good wishes and messages to family members abroad. We also received messages from abroad and in my teenage years it fell to me to deliver those on my bicycle when the Postman was not around. Christmas Eve was an extremely busy day for us with the combination of customers in the shop and telegrams to be delivered. In terms of workload, the two weeks before Christmas were always 14 hour days or more for us.

The Post Office Years

At the age of 14 years, I was working in the post office and the little shop attached full time. The shop stocked newspapers, schools supplies and household supplies. There was a small pallet placed in front of the counter on which I would stand so that I would seem older to the customers. Over the next few years Jeanie's health declined. Eventually she suffered a stroke and wasn't able to work anymore. Along the way we had added food items which we expanded later.

At the age of 21, I took over management of the post office which lasted for 20 years. It was an experience that was a great preparation for life. The post office, like the church, the creamery and the pub, were the social centres of the rural community. We had a chair in the post office, frequently a cup of tea and scone. People would want to sit, have a chat, talk about issues in their lives, an illness, the son or daughter's schooling; 'will we be able to pay for the education?' Life was simple in the forties. There was real poverty in the rural communities. Work was extremely scarce. Husbands went away to find work in Dublin or in England. Wives cared for the children and worked the land. The great pity was the continuous loss of young people shortly after leaving school. They had no choice but to leave home. In farming, it was usually the eldest son who was kept home to work on the farm and eventually take it over. All other siblings left, most of whom emigrated. I think only four or five of my class at school remained at home. Of those that left the majority went to England to work. They would come home mostly in summer for two weeks. I would meet them in the post office and a short chat would ensue. Many worked in Birmingham and Coventry, making components for the motor industry. Poverty of course was relevant; it was a matter of degree of poverty and the willpower of the individual to make ends meet. In our area, it was not as difficult as it was in other parts of the country. Our proximity to Dublin City was important. Farmers all grew their own food and non-farmers also had good gardens which meant that nobody was hungry, provided they worked their holdings

Marriage to Paddy

My move to Clonalvy had another beneficial outcome as there I met a local man, Patrick (Paddy) McGuinness, a local farmer's son. Our friendship started when I was 17 and we were married when I was 19. Our first child came when I was 21. We had six children - Jean, Gerard, Annie, Margo, Pat and Michelle.

Unfortunately Jeanie had passed away before we were married. In the early years, we lived above the post office. The children growing up attracted another range of visitors to the post office, they had their own friends and I found young mothers wanted to share experiences.

Paddy inherited his father's farm and later another farm came on the market very close to the Post Office which we bought. In the sixties, there was a great deal of media engagement on Ireland joining the Common Market, now the E.U. There was a plan called the Mansholt Plan, named after Sicco Mansholt, former President of the European Commission, for the development of agriculture and the EU food market.

This plan was promising big benefits for farmers, recommending greater output and increased productivity on farms. The prediction was that farm sizes would have to increase so as to be viable. What would that mean, more investment, more borrowings, higher livestock numbers, more machinery and farm buildings. Would it provide for, or leave room for traditional organic farming? That never appeared in print or in radio or TV discussion. What would be the impact on food supplies, food quality and the environment? Forty years on, I am firmly of the belief that whilst E.U. membership and its policies were good for Ireland and beneficial in general, the overall impact on public health and the planet has been damaging.

Paddy and I agreed that we would stay as close as possible to traditional farming and food production. We avoided going the intensive farming route of more livestock, high levels of fertilization, expensive buildings and increased slurry and waste. However, we had to be enterprising to meet the needs of a growing family. To supplement our income, we conceived the idea of making leather wallets, handbags, and light household items. Paddy would travel to sell the goods to gift and souvenir shops and seaside stands during the summer months. The expansion of the shop had continued immediately after we got married. We added homemade bread and other foods. At Christmas we would make about 80 Christmas cakes and maybe 20 Plum Puddings. That practice continued up to the end of the sixties but by then the Supermarkets had arrived and they supplied cakes nicely wrapped in red paper and ribbons.

Paddy and I had a great life together and we shared a lot in common. Neither of us smoked or drank alcohol. That helped us with savings, which went into the education of our children. We purchased a camper van when the children were young and as a family we travelled together. Festivals and musical events were major attractions. We also used to go on camping trips to Carlingford every year. We did the Carlingford trip for 47 years. At weekends especially in good weather we would drive to the seaside for a day, usually to Laytown, just to walk on the beach. Farming was always described as a seven day job but by planning and sharing everyone can have time off. Every week we made sure we had some time for ourselves together and every year we made sure to take some time out on the road. I have wonderful memories of our camping trips together.

After the family had grown up, Paddy and I continued that practice. We met interesting people around the country and we covered all four provinces, focusing on seaside resorts. Both Paddy and I became Red Cross Volunteers. We were both ambulance drivers and in addition, I did all the essential training for handling emergencies.

We attended football and hurling matches, race meetings, festivals and fleadh ceoils, marches, parades and pilgrimages to Knock. In those years we did not have the Health and Safety Regulations like we have today, but we did have standby and emergency services many of which were on a voluntary basis. We witnessed and assisted with many happenings, from the joy of premature births to the misery of excess alcohol. We provided first aid after alcohol-fuelled fights and brawls, attended road accidents and in some cases emergency room treatments.

We were members of the Red Cross for forty years, but after I started practice I had to curtail my availability. The Red Cross provided a very important service to the community and depended heavily on charitable donations. I was honoured to be invited to organise a high-profile fundraising event in the National Concert Hall specifically to raise funds for a new ambulance.

The camper van had another use. Bernard McGuinness, Paddy's father or Grandad as we called him, was a very religious man with great faith. He loved to go to Knock every year for a pilgrimage. Paddy and I joined in and followed his example. In fact, we became so committed that for about 30 years Paddy and I went to Knock every Easter for the 3 day festivities. I found it was a great spiritual lift which renewed my spirits. We parked on a space alongside others within the Bassilica area, the Church as it was in the early years. The late Monsignor Horan was the man who made such an impact on the development of the Shrine at Knock. On one occasion, he came over to our van and asked if we were comfortable. After chatting for a few minutes he looked around and then said, we must improve the parking facilities for pilgrims. When we came back next year, the plot was levelled and gravelled. Progressively over a few years it was improved. When I first heard on the radio he was looking to build an airport at Knock for the West of Ireland, I felt immediately he would realise that dream. He was a visionary, a man of the people and an achiever.

I was also fortunate to travel to Lourdes on a few occasions. I went with the Dublin Franciscan Pilgrimage as a helper. Like Knock, it was a marvellous experience and a striking image remains with me, the deep faith people have in the power of God.

Grandad, suffered from a stroke and had difficulties with recovery. His wife had died when the children were teenagers so he had been through hard times. He came to live with us as all his family had left home. He spent the last 14 years of his life with us. Despite needing a wheelchair to get around, he was no bother. He was great company and so we got on really well together.

Agnes and Paddy with the family on their 50th wedding anniversary.
From left: Michelle, Annie, Paddy, Gerard, Pat, Agnes, Margo and Jean.

We were also lifelong members of the GAA. This organisation throughout my lifetime, together with ceili music and the Church were the core elements of life in Ireland, especially the rural communities. The Church was pivotal in the community, it was the key organiser of education and either owned or controlled most of the hospitals. The GAA organised the sporting facilities especially the clubs which developed a community fabric in which friendships were developed entertainment was provided, romances enabled and healthy rivalry was processed through competitive sport. During the 90s football in Meath was at its best. There was a great rivalry with Dublin and when they won in Leinster then Kerry became the team to beat. Paddy was an ardent supporter and so was Gerard. Most Sundays of the year they were away when Meath were playing.

We were regulars at and loved going ceili dancing and meeting other people. The Seamus Ennis Band was best known in our home area and was well supported. County Clare was the recognised leader for traditional music. We travelled many a weekend to Ennis where we parked the camper. From there we would travel out to a parish hall to hear the Tulla or Kilfenora Ceili Bands playing. It was delightful.

As the decades passed, television sports created new interest for the younger generation. Soccer became popular for teenagers and young men. Our grandchildren and their friends played it in addition to Gaelic football. To enhance their facilities, Paddy took an interest in local soccer development. I was delighted later on when Cloghertown FC named their new grounds, McGuinness Park in honour of Paddy and his contribution to the club in its early years.

Four generations of McGuinness Family, at christening of Emily.
Great Grandmother Agnes with baby Emily, dad Pat and grandad Gerard.

Empathy with People

Normal practice in the community was to help neighbours in times of need. One example was the midwife who assisted during home birthing. In the early part of the last century, most births were at home. A local midwife attended and provided follow-up care for mother and baby. Such a person was not necessarily medically trained but had that innate ability and connection with people; their presence was sought by the individual mother-to-be and indeed the family. I recall my first delivery of a baby, when I was called urgently to come to a neighbour's house to assist in the birth of their child. All was successfully achieved before the ambulance arrived, right down to wrapping the afterbirth in newspaper.

Likewise, at the other end of life, we had people - women - who attended neighbours at their time of death. Their presence was important to the dying and the family. It was a healing touch, probably derived from the empathetic approach of the provider. I was about 17 when I had my first experience of attending to the recently deceased. The community senior at the time was in the post office one day and said she was going in an hour or two to the home of a lady who had just died. She was going to lay her out and prepare her for the wake.

The wake was an event always held in the family home on the evening after the person had passed away. Neighbours and friends came to extend their condolences, many ended up as a late-night party with spirits and snuff. I attended at the laying out and was shown how to wash the body, make up the hair and get the deceased suitably dressed and laid out on their bed. As time progressed, I was asked directly by a number of families to attend to their family member who had passed away and to prepare them for their wake and coffining. I found after a while it came easy to me, as if I had a natural talent. Another case I recall is that of an elderly man. He mentioned his age and said 'sur I haven't long to go, but I want you to be the person who closes my eyes for the last time'. I laughed and said 'it will have to be a Sunday, Jim, because I'm so busy here in this Post Office'. A few months later I got a message that Jim was not well. He was attended by the doctor early in the week and was expected to pass on within 24 hours. The following Sunday morning, Jim died at 7am. I got the feeling that I should have taken him more seriously when we had last talked.

I think he waited for me to be available for his passing.

An elderly couple Willie and Katie lived about two miles from our home. They used to come into the post office to collect their pensions and buy some household items.

I got to know Katie very well and over the years we built up a rapport. One day Katie was on my mind, pretty much all day. I had not seen her come in for a week or more. That evening after closing, I cycled over to their home. Willie was outside the door and he said as I got off my bicycle 'Katie is upstairs; she is not feeling too good'. I talked to Katie for a minute or two, then washed her and brushed her hair as she requested. Then I put a fresh nightdress on Katie and put fresh bedlinen on the bed. I said 'Katie, I think those sheets are a little damp'. She protested and said 'anything wrapped in brown paper is never damp'. Once that was done, she was resting as I tidied up. Then Katie said 'Agnes'. That was her last word, she passed away immediately. I closed her eyes and her mouth then said a prayer for the repose of her soul. I went downstairs to tell Willie. He was still out in the garden and I said 'Willie, Katie has passed away.' He turned around slowly, and after a second he just responded with the words, "she had been hoping that you would be the person who would close her eyes for the last time."

I felt humbled and as I cycled back home I was tearful. I felt lonely for the next few days until after Katie's funeral. I realised that, two people whom I had known for nearly a decade, who were 50 years older than me, were not just customers but they were my friends. No wonder I was tearful, but it gave me confidence in myself. I remembered that friendship for years and it encouraged me further.

Chapter Two

Training & Practice

Healthcare and Training

My formal schooling had been cut short by the early death of my mother. For years after, I felt a great desire to educate myself. In later years, I would say to myself, I would love to have been a doctor if the opportunity had arisen. Soon after we were married, I bought with Paddy's agreement, an Encyclopaedia of Medical Books, which I paid for on a monthly basis. At that time, it was called hire purchase, same procedure that people used to buy their cars. My confidence was growing, helped along by the many discussions and interactions with people in the Post Office and the neighbourhood requests for help. Something was telling me that I had a wider contribution to make.

It was 1963 when I saw an advertisement for a course on anatomy and physiology in Trinity College. It was two evenings per week, costing 10 shillings per evening, running for one year. It was costly, but the build-up within me of wanting to serve people with their healthcare needs was strong. The experience as a Red Cross assistant combined with the many unofficial consultations in the post office had built up my confidence. I enrolled in the course and completed the year. Towards the end of the course, a young doctor, then an intern, told me that another more advanced course would be available soon on the North Circular Road. The venue had been a convent but I don't know what it is used as today. The course was run by an English organisation and was given over a six-month period. Fifty six (56) students enrolled on that course. I completed the examination at the end. We had to wait two weeks for the results, which I thought at the time were the longest two weeks of my life. When the results came, I was placed fourth in the exam. The doctor who had told me about it said 'I knew you could do it, you should have been first.

Bone Structure

These courses fuelled my thirst for knowledge - my interest in health was always great - and set me on a path to learn as much as I could about biology and the body. Now I wanted to know more about bones and muscular structure, I found such a course in Exeter in the UK and booked a place. There was a small attendance. It was led by an Orthopaedic Surgeon. On the first day, he grimaced a few times and mentioned his sore knee. After a while I spoke to him about it and he responded that it was arthritis coming on. I suggested that if he got rid of his constipation his sore knee would also go away. He said, what do you mean, rather gruffly. I suggested he take Epsom salts and drink two litres of water per day.

He obviously did, as on Friday morning he came in carrying three books, slapped them down on the desk and said, take these, you have no medical training yet you cleared my constipation and my sore knee in two days. He may not have been very pleasant with his gruff manner, but his heart was in the right place and his teaching in skeletal health was good.

Training for Practice

Within a few weeks of starting my course in Trinity, people - mostly neighbours - were coming to ask me questions. In country areas, neighbours always know what is going on, and that's a good thing for the most part. The word was out; Agnes is doing a course in Trinity. 'What is she doing? I think it's some medical course.' Some would congratulate me and lead on to ask what I was doing. Before long they were looking for a little information, some help for themselves. It was not unlike the chats in the Post Office over the years, but it was a little more formal. However, the conversation could be in the post office, after mass on Sunday, during a walk on the road or anywhere.

- **Constipation** was the complaint that came up most, 'I have it permanently'. I would ask 'do you drink water?'; 'not much, no'. I recommended drinking two pints a day or more.

- **Headache or Migraine** – 'I have it constantly' or 'it comes and goes regularly'. 'What's your food like, what do you eat, do you drink water?' At that point, the answers become vague, yes and no to the same question.

- **Fatigue** - 'I am tired all the time, you know, not enough energy. I would ask 'what do you do, what do you work at? What's your sleep like?' 'Oh, I am working in Dublin, drive in every day'. My response was that it may be connected with their diet, foods that weren't agreeing with them, or even perhaps their work.

- **Menses** - periods were irregular, painful or non-existent for some women. Comments like, 'my mother says she never had these problems when she was my age.' What did I think is wrong? There could be any number of answers.

I was still a student and still working in the Post Office. The number of casual enquirers/well-wishers was sending me a message. What was the message? What did many of these people have in common? Most were women, although a few men introduced their question through congratulations. I loved both the course in Trinity and the second course on the North Circular Road. I had wanted to do that type of study for almost twenty years. Now the questions people were asking, caused me to ask myself, did I do the right course. Yes, was the answer to myself, I did it for me. But the people out there had other needs that were not covered in the anatomy and physiology courses which had taken up nearly two years of my life. I had to do more study.

What did all those people with the above and other questions or ailments have in common? These were people mostly from my own neighbourhood. Many of them would have known me personally and some were the next generation, young adults. The younger generation were now perhaps living in the area and working in Dublin. Some lived in Dublin and travelled back at weekends. The daily travel was a factor; dehydration, stress, dinner in the evening, fast food. Lifestyle was an issue. It contributed in some way to all of the conditions mentioned above. There were other conditions that people wanted also to discuss. Contraception was a big issue in Ireland at the time. The Church was opposed to artificial contraception. Young women in their twenties were confused. Mothers or grannies or both were also opposed. Some went to the priest in confession. Priests were sending out mixed messages; some a clear no, others said if the doctor had recommended it for health reasons, then it was ok. Some people sought my opinions. I don't know why but that was life.

source: iStock.com/pepifoto

More Training Required

The first 15 years of practice I worked principally with herbs, diet, exercise and personal advice. But I found that lifestyle changes bring about life changes. Living in a flat or bedsit in Dublin meant a diet different to what people had experienced at home. The word *allergy* was new to public conversation. It was not in the medical textbooks. I knew it was an area I had to learn more about. Another course beckoned.

Bio-Energy Assessment was a procedure I heard about which had been developed by a priest, Fr Freddie Fox. The course was held in Stillorgan, Co Dublin and was presented by Sr Rachel Hoey. I signed up for that course and found it very interesting. Indeed, the personal story of Fr Fox was interesting.

Reflexology was another energy medicine technique that I signed up for. Reflexology is a science based on the principle that points in the feet and hands correspond and connect with specific organs and glands. By massaging or activating those points, you can influence the wellbeing of the particular organ.

The Pendulum

Dowsing was used by some practitioners in my early years. However, dowsing has been with us down through the ages. A pendulum can be as simple is as a weight on a piece of string. You can also buy crystal, metal or glass preparations. It's a question of what suits you best. The pendulum is a very useful tool for the therapist alongside kinesiology or computerised devices as it allows a second check when certain issues arise in the clinic. You can conduct distance therapy when a client calls on the phone and is in need of guidance. I continue to use my pendulum almost every day. If the client is fatigued or in need of rest I can scan a range of organs that need testing without his/her active involvement whereas when using kinesiology the client must be involved.

Vega Testing

Dr George Lewith a doctor in Southampton provided the training on Vega Testing in Dublin. He recommended the use of a little machine, then called the VGT Test, later renamed Vega Test. It was German technology and had been in use there for a long time. Dr Lewith had practiced conventional medicine for nearly 20 years but found it was not meeting the needs of his patients so he changed over to natural therapies.

The course concentrated on food sensitivity. Using homeopathic vials of specific foods, the machine enabled you to test whether or not that food was suitable or unsuitable for the client. It mattered not what the food was.

A 'good food' such as tomatoes, cherries or cabbage, whilst good for the public at large might be unsuitable for a specific individual. It varied from person to person. Some might be sensitive to just one food item or several. This brought us to another level; what brought about this situation? Why is a tomato not suitable for one person when it is fine for their sister, brother or neighbour? There was further enquiry and further learning to be done. I purchased the Vega machine. I believe it was the first in the country, and I still have it, still use it and it meets my needs. In the forty years that have elapsed, several new computerised versions and other new devices have emerged.

I found on the job training the best method of learning. More people were coming for advice. I had to make a decision: did I give up the post office and start a new profession? Paddy became my advisor. I had to look at it as a new business. I had always known in my heart that I wanted to help people so I was now at a crossroads. Did I help them as the local post mistress or did I help them with their health issues and all that it entailed? Along the way, we had built a new house on the land we had purchased. Paddy converted a room for me to use as a therapy room. There I started with my Vega device. My stock of books became even bigger. With more experience came a greater quest for knowledge.

A few years later we added three rooms which Paddy described as the granny flat. I used this space as my clinic and these rooms remain in use today.

Kinesiology became my next focus. I had read about it, the information available sounded good and so it turned out to be. I was able to find a course in Dublin run by Risteard De Barra who had trained in the International Kinesiology College in Switzerland and was now teaching Touch for Health (TFH). This programme was devised by an American doctor John Thie, as an entry point to kinesiology. Dr Thie designed it for home-use, advocating the concept of people taking more responsibility for their personal health and that of their families. Dr John Diamond used kinesiology extensively in his practice and conducted a great deal therapeutic applications.*

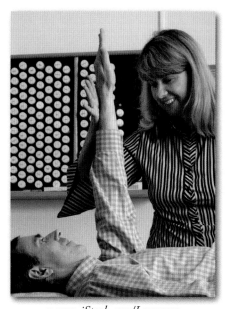

source: iStock.com/Leezsnow

* **Your Body Doesn't Lie** - *John Diamond, M.D / Grand Central life & Style - Hachette Book Group   ISBN 0-446-35847-9*

The classroom element of TFH was four months with a follow-up, and home study and revision covering another four months. Essentially, the same as a school year. The training was very good as was the outcome. I was able to utilise it alongside my Vega machine and use muscle testing to test outcomes from the Vega machine and vice versa.

Herbs were always of interest to me, as they were to my mother, so it was herbs I used most when my clients needed extra therapy. Jan de Vries was a Herbalist and teacher so I attended his lectures when he came to Dublin which he did regularly. He was very interesting and had a great deal of knowledge on herbs for medicinal use. Apart from the herbs he would tell us about life in his home country of Holland in his childhood. Holland was occupied by the Germans during the war years and life was not easy, food and many household needs were rationed or not available. My recollection of our shortages in Ireland was only a fraction of the difficulties they had in Holland.

PRANA was the next level of training in kinesiology. This was an advanced and more specific branch of kinesiology which focused on a number of issues, but two that specifically interested me at that time were nutrition and emotional health.

Angela Burr-Madsen, led the course. She was a practitioner and teacher in natural medicines for more than a decade and had a wealth of practical stories to share from practice. PRANA, is an acronym for *Polarity Reflex Analysis and Nutritional Assessment*. It took testing to a new level. Angela used the term *Vital Force*. I had first heard those words in relation to homeopathy, where the founder of that medical system stated that it was core to the health of the individual. Now it was used in relation to foods, the *Vital Force* of the food. PRANA asked very relevant questions. What was the level of *Vital Force* of the individual food? Did the VF of the food on the shelf match that of the organic food from the farm? Did the VF of the food match the health needs of the client? Individual body chemistry was an issue, foods that suited the individual, foods that did not, could all be measured.

Another aspect of this course was the role of the subconscious mind. Some writers now refer to this as *the unconscious mind*. It plays a critical role in our lives, particularly quality of life. This I found, was a crucial benefit of kinesiology. It helped explain why I was finding so many emotional issues in the clients coming to see me. By the end of the course, I had come to understand that the foods we eat impact on our brain, feelings, emotions, energy, outlook, memory and more.

It is now referred to in clinical journals as *the gut-brain connection*. Two words in particular stood out in my mind at that point; *Toxin and Deficiency*. For more information, see Kinesiology: Communication with the Subconscious.*

Iridology

Iridology is a method of identifying problems in the body through the appearance of the eyes. I was looking for more diagnostic procedures to help me identify problems which people were presenting with and I found this course very interesting. Kinesiology and Vega Testing gave me direct results using a commodity, a food, supplement or remedy. Now I wanted to see if the body itself reflected the inner strength, deficiency or a trouble spot. The doctor who presented this course, whose name I cannot recall now, was an outstanding speaker and teacher. He referred  very frequently to Traditional Chinese Medicine (TCM) and the Meridians. The meridians are effectively energy pathways throughout the body through which the energy flows and provides health and vitality to the cells. Each meridian is associated with an organ so you can test the health of the organ by pressing on the relative meridian.

Influential Healers and Colleagues

I have no doubt that there were many natural and local healers in communities everywhere throughout the course of history. Only a few of the great names or innovators will have been passed on to us through books and libraries. I mention names such as Hippocrates, Aristotle, Paracelsus, Samuel Hahnemann and Rudolf Steiner. Those were people who were the sages, scientists and visionaries of their time. I came to look at people of modern times including my own time, and here I found many who left a legacy which included priests, religious sisters and lay people alike.

---

* **Kinesiology** - *The diagnostic tool to identify information and messages from the sub-conscious. Angela Burr Madsen. Positive Health Online. Issue 219. Dec 2014.*

Fr Freddie Fox was a Divine Word Missionary Priest, an American national who had difficulties with his personal health. Conventional medicine did not provide relief so he turned to his own resources and looked at *"energy medicine"*. He took on board therapies like reflexology, acupuncture, colour and magnetic therapy. He found these therapies effective in different ways as standalone techniques. He started to combine them as needs arose and from his research he developed a practice called *Bio-Energy Therapy*. He added other modules such as homeopathy, Traditional Chinese Medicine (TCM) and MORA therapy. As a true missionary he travelled to many countries, ministering to people as a Priest, which was his first calling, but also teaching how they could best help themselves from a personal health viewpoint.

Sr Rachel Hoey, a Mercy Order Sister came to know of the work of Fr Fox and asked him if he would come to Ireland to teach students his healing techniques. The true missionary was happy to do so and for those who were fortunate to want to know more it was a rewarding experience, myself included.

Sr Rachel herself has been a great teacher and healer for more than three decades. She was followed by many other people of like mind whose only aim was to help people the best way they knew how. Other colleagues with whom I shared great training time were Sisters Lydwina Farrell and Helen McKenna. Like Sr Rachel, Lydwina and Helen were wholly committed to healing and helping. The role of The Church was now becoming obvious, committed people presenting in a new light, quite unlike the structured Church that I had known in my first forty years of life.

Angela Burr Madsen, was an Irish lady who lived and worked in California. She was an amazing teacher who could hold the attention of her classroom or any audience for a full day and they still wanted more. In her practice, people were coming in whom she found very toxic, not just from the regular environmental nasties like chemicals and metals but also foods and health foods. In an effort to overcome problems people took high dose Vitamin C, various herbs and minerals as they were available from health shops and pharmacies. But the timing was wrong, the body was not able to absorb such rich commodities. Already toxic they were now adding to their toxic load. Angela used homeopathic preparations of the items she identified with her kinesiology to detox these nutrients and then did a layered detox of the other items identified. She used the phrase, *peel the onion back one layer at a time*. Students related to this and it helped their understanding.

Apart from the kinesiology training, Angela was a mine of information. The ten years of practice and the experience she had gained was a huge help to students. She shared it so generously and she was so interesting with her style of delivery and presentation. She told us about trends in the United States. Overweight people including children, were in the majority in her practice and she had linked this to the food chain and the supply chain. The outdoor takeaway had become very much the norm in America by then. But what she found most disturbing was the level of consumption of fizzy drinks. A bottle of Coke or Fanta was the normal school lunch drink for the previous 10 years or more. It was showing in individual behaviour, (bad behaviour) in emotional health and in the waistline. Soft sugary drinks were promoted at filling stations at reduced costs and were stacked on the outside, right alongside the pumps. They were available in plastic bottles, larger in size than what we had at that time, with packs of 12 or 24 bottles shrink wrapped. At that point in 1990, the Naturopathic Society in California of which Angela was a member were canvassing the State Governor to introduce regulations to prevent the oil companies from promoting Fizzy Drinks on Forecourts because of the damage being done to the health of children and adults alike.

Angela made two visits to Ireland every ear to give training seminars whilst Sr Rachel continued with her courses, most of which were held at St Raphiels Convent in Stillorgan. We had other visiting lecturers introduced by various companies. We had a great sense of purpose and confidence in the late 1980s and early 1990s. Companionship built up. We were all learning together and of course numbers were small. Dr Hillary Webb was Dublin based GP and he was moving his practice exclusively towards natural therapies. Other colleagues, Patricia Quinn, Padraig Toner, Rosaleen Kelly, Olive Hayes, Pat Roche and Robyn Smyth were all members of the training seminars, so we had the opportunity to meet regularly and share opinions. Both Dr Webb and Padraig Toner died at young ages and both were a big loss to the natural health movement.

As practices built up we got busy and it was not as easy then to take time out or meet, so I missed that. Sr Rachel had replaced Fr Freddie as President of the BTTI which had a mission of promoting bio-testing at home and abroad. To meet the needs of the expanding portfolio of practice skills the Naturopathic Society was established. Rosaleen Kelly gave time and energy to its mission.
I encourage all practitioners to meet regularly and share information and knowledge. You will benefit personally and so will your clients. In the early years The Spa Hotel in Lucan was the venue most often used for conferences and lectures, it provided great service at affordable costs to our movement.
For almost fifteen (15) years we ran evening courses in the clinic, one evening per week for eight (8) weeks.

I enjoyed that aspect as it required a different engagement with the participants than with clients. After Lorna left I had to give up the teaching as it was too much of a workload.

Martin Murray founded the New Vistas Laboratory which was a huge boost to natural health services in Ireland, so I consider Mr Murray as a key contributor to our sector. Supply of products and training is now much improved compared to the early 1980s. Previously I had used Tissue Salts and Herbs from the UK and I imported Blackmores Mineral Salts from Australia. New Vistas brought a new dimension with specific detoxification remedies for the toxic times we live in. The organ remedies called Liquescences (short for liquid essences) are novel in their preparation combining vitamins, minerals and herbs. They heal stressed organs and also are ideal health tonics that have helped thousands of people over the years. Mineral supplements are difficult to absorb and assimilate and up to 90% of the individual supplement can be excreted from the body before absorption. In the Liquescence format they are the genuine micro-nutrient and therefore are more suited to organs which are burdened and stressed by toxins and other injuries. Whilst Mr Murray does not see clients personally, through the products and services his company provided to the practitioner community, his contributions to health and healing had been enormous.

Thomas Haberle. I was lucky to find a delightful little book, *Helping and Healing* by Thomas Haberle, first published in German in 1984. Unfortunately it is not still available, unless you are fortunate to find a second hand copy. Thomas Haberle was a Swiss National, a Benedictine Priest. In his early years of religious life he spent nearly 20 years as a teacher, physics and mathematics. In addition he was assigned the task of providing retreats and novenas for parishes, schools or colleges throughout the country. He recalls one such retreat he had to give in the south of the country close to the Italian border. He had the good fortune to have his roof and board provided at a Monastery in the locality. There he made the acquaintance of an elderly Monk who had retired from active ministry but enjoyed his time tending to the Monastery Garden. From that garden he fed the monastic community and many others in need throughout the year. Fr Haberle described himself as fascinated by the knowledge and enthusiasm that the elderly cleric displayed especially the healing power he attributed to many of the plants and herbs in his garden.

His enthusiasm went further when he saw this monk use his pendulum. As a science teacher he had heard of a pendulum, but did or could a scientist use a pendulum. His mentor was only too keen to demonstrate. He explained and demonstrated how you could identify good quality soil, balanced soil nutrition and so on, why a person suffered from certain ailments or illnesses.

On his return to his normal job, his real preoccupation was, how could he acquire the knowledge and skill his new found colleague spoke so eloquently about.

As he settled into his new school year his new interest was natural healing. Now he was reading about names like Pastor Kunzle and Pastor Kneipp. He found there was a strong Church engagement in healing by churchmen with very credible reputations. He was teaching science by day and studying nature in the evening. |Soon he realised there was no conflict. He had a new dimension to his calling, he still wanted to help people with their issues: now he realised there was a connection between their spiritual and religious needs and their temporal and health needs. Getting back to visit the Monastery and spending time with his mentor was a priority. He achieved that and his first lesson was, go to the garden test all the plants with your pendulum and list them in order of healing priority. He was on his way towards being a healer.

Soon after he applied to his superiors for a transfer from teaching and into parish ministry. There he could connect directly with people and view at first hand their needs. His wish was granted and he was assigned the role as Parish Priest in a rural part of the country in the foothills of the Alps.

Now parted from the confines of monastic life he was in direct contact with people. He used his pendulum to assess their symptoms so as to identify the causes of their condition.

In the 40 years that followed he treated thousands of people. He summarises his findings in his book and lists some of the problems and his solutions. These included:

• **Geopathic Stress,** and no real surprise in that the territory was mountainous and was therefore prone to underground caverns and streams, many as much as 30 meters below the surface. Furthermore to enhance and keep housing costs lower many families had home basements build into the land which they used as storage space. As technology improved, boilers, coolers, pumps and other machinery was installed. All of these impacted on sleep and essential rejuvenation and set people on a downward health course. He was able to advise on solutions like moving the bed and also devise solutions like copper coils for under the mattress.

• **Diet** was another issue especially the overuse of animal fats. When he visited schools as part of his parochial duty he could identify from the aroma and smell of the air that animal slaughter was underway on the farms. This was Advent time and due to suppressed immune systems higher levels of winter colds and flu would follow. Same followed for several weeks after the spring slaughter, but with summer and more sunshine available it was not as severe.

However, he noted enlargements in the neck with swollen lymph nodes resulting from the fat. This effected the liver and gallbladder and was a key cause of tuberculosis. Education was key.

- He used fresh cabbage leaves as a healing procedure for many issues that troubled people like cysts, abscess external and internal, blisters, pimples, inflamed skin, broken tissue, bed sores and wounds from other activities. Placing a fresh leaf or leaves overnight drew out the abscess and fluid.

- Olive oil was another favoured treatment for a variety of ailments like rheumatism, joint pain, stiffness, bone marrow problems, inflammation and head disorders. Rub in the oil to the affected area, leave for two minutes, before you wipe it off. The oil penetrates the skin.

- He combined fresh cabbage treatment with olive oil, with the cabbage poultice used overnight followed by the oil treatment in the morning.

- Salt was another of his favoured treatments, rubbed in after the olive oil treatment but on a controlled basis and for certain conditions.

- Clay baths and ordinary water baths were also important but he advised that baths should be neither too hot nor too long.

Fr Haberle makes a point in his book of having refused to treat cancers, unless the person also worked with their doctor in tandem. Many were happy to do this. He would not use the olive oil treatment as he felt the oil could move the cancer from one organ to another. All special and individual advice or recommendation given to people was based on guidance from his Pendulum.

He saw the pendulum as a gift from God, therefore sacred and had to be treated as such. He found direct connection with the teachings of the early Church with what he was doing. On cancer treatments, whilst he held back on the body care he advised and counselled on the emotional aspects and the role of the soul in illness. Again he found the parallels in scripture and the passages in the gospels.*

Emanuel Felke was another remarkable healer in Germany. Felke was a Pastor in the protestant community and his final posting in his lifetime was to a community located on the river Rhur right in the heart of Germanys industrially developed Rhur Valley region. Felke was a naturopath who used traditional herbs as well as clay baths, sun baths, detoxification procedures, exercise, diet and spiritual counselling for his clientele. He was strong on our connection with the Earth and Planet. No surprise he had clay as an important part of his therapeutic program. For that reason he was affectionately known as the Clay Pastor.

---

* **Helping and Healing**- *Thomas Haberle, Sheldon Press ISBN 0-85969-528-X*

Our connection with the Earth, and the role it plays in health is outlined by Marijke Vogel in her book *The Earth on which we live.**

Was it divine providence that led his Church to send him to this location. The Region was going through change with heavy industry having started 50 years earlier. Young people, but also mature people also, left the farms and villages of the South and East and flocked to the North West to work 60 hour weeks in coal mines, foundries, railway carriage assembly and other engineering establishments. The lifestyle change and associated dietary issues soon brought changes in health and wellbeing. Medical care of the time did not meet the new challenges.

Felke, with a different approach, a pastoral approach, a guiding and helping approach was recognised and supported. He raised funds, bought some land and step by step build built up recuperation and recovery units around a large treatment centre. At first it was all traditional naturopathic treatment but then he came to know homeopathy which he tried. He set up a small preparation laboratory and following Samuel Hahnemanns teachings he made up his own remedies matched to the needs of his patients. It was a great success and he was later to report that homeopathy became the backbone of his clinic.**
I could relate to that as it was very similar to my own experience in practice.

Training of other practitioners became another aspect of Pastor Felke's service such that within 25 years of starting practice, some 30 Felke Societies had been established around the North and East of Germany. Three of his personal patients did so well following his treatments that on recovery they decided to train as practitioners. They opened and ran successful practices and their children between them started up four (4) homeopathic production companies which continue as worldwide suppliers today. What a legacy.

---

* **The Earth on which we live** - *Marijke Vogel, Vogel and Vogel, ISBN0-9540693-0-7*
** **Pathways of Homeopathic Medicine** – *Dr. Bettina Blessing, ISBN 978-3-642-14970-2 Springer.de*

Chapter Three

People's Health Complaints

Toxicity

Deficiencies relate to nutritional deficiencies. I was well aware from my childhood years of the importance of good nutrition; I learned of its importance from my mother. Deficiencies were somewhat new to me and how they came about. The connection between toxicity and deficiencies was what I wanted to know more about, so that became the next phase of my quest for knowledge. Toxins were emerging and interfering with people's lives and they arose from a range of sources and were varied in nature. Chief among those were:

Chemicals which came from fertilizers spread on the land, with run-off into rivers and lakes, contaminating the food chain through water and fish. Weedkillers, pesticides and crop spraying were other sources of chemicals which people came in contact with, absorbed through the skin and inhaled through breathing. There were no protective masks available in those times as we have today.

The impact of those chemicals on natural ecosystems, the destruction caused to plant animal and bird life by the indiscriminate use of those chemicals combined with the potential risk to human health was for the first time brought home to the public by Dr. Rachel Carson in a ground breaking and profoundly important book *Silent Spring*. Bird song had been wiped out in so many places. Dr. Carson's book made the public and Governments aware of the potential risks to health from the uncontrolled use of those chemicals.* I recall in the 1960s we sprinkled DDT liberally across door saddles and on window sills to keep the flies and bugs out. Even the cat and dog were dusted. Likewise, chemical sprays such as Duter arrived to replace the traditional bluestone and washing soda mix which had been used to control potato blight. A host of other new chemical products emerged to control weeds, best known of which was Roundup. This product contained a base chemical called glyphosate which I found was highly toxic when I resonance tested people.

Following publication of *Silent Spring*, an enquiry was established in the United States to look into the use of pesticides and other chemicals. As a result of the enquiry many of those chemicals were removed from the market. I would think that it wasn't that all of them were bad in themselves, it was the indiscriminate and widespread use which was a key part of the problem. Pursuit of profit causes that to happen.

Emissions from factories, chemical plants, disposal of waste, the burning of rubber and other issues all had an adverse impact on the environment which further impacted on people's lives through inhalation to the lungs.

---

* **Silent Spring** - *Dr Rachel Carson. Houghton Mifflin Company. ISBN 0-618-24906-0.*

Home furnishings such as mattresses, couches and carpets contained formaldehyde and were treated with pesticides and other chemicals such that people were in almost constant contact with chemical compounds. Dr. Sherry Rogers outlines the adverse impact on health such exposures can have such as neurodegenerative disorders and cancers*. These products impacted on all body systems and altered our DNA leaving us susceptible to a host of adverse health conditions.

Fluoride in the water was another source of chemicals. This process of fluoridation of drinking water was introduced to prevent tooth cavities, which is also referred to as dental caries. The outcomes for dental health is very questionable with dental fluorosis becoming a common problem. This is a colouring of the enamel of the tooth also referred to as mottled enamel. The fluoride that is added to the water is very toxic. It is a bye product of fertilizer, specifically phosphate production. It contains heavy metals like arsenic, lead, cadmium and silica. These compounds when they make their way into the body will accumulate and result later in, bone and brain disorders and cancers. For more information read Barry Groves, *Fluoride, Drinking ourselves to death.* **

Chlorine is another chemical added to water, especially swimming pools. The intention is the kill harmful bacteria so that people avoid infection. The only problem is that excess chlorine in the water or excess exposure to chlorine is a problem for people and especially for those that are sensitive. Skin conditions arise and the chlorine with other bio-accumulative chemicals are an increased cancer risk.

Food additives have become a feature of the food supply as traditional food preparation has been abandoned, replaced instead by industrially processed foods. These additives were all chemical in nature and used as preservatives, taste enhancers, colouring and shelf life enhancers. As people had gone over more and more to processed foods, I found that daily ingestion had brought about accumulation of these compounds in the body. Those compounds were bio-accumulative, they stored in tissue, in organs and made their way to cells. They are transported by the blood stream around the body, they clog up the connective tissue and prevent nutrient distribution to the cells. No surprise then that thirty years later that we have new blood health conditions like *porphyria, Gilberts syndrome* or *bilirubin* all of which are invisible, but nevertheless there are problems in storage which will manifest later.***

---

*   **Tired or Toxic** - *Dr Sherry Rodgers MD. Prestige Publishing . ISBN 0-9618821-2-*
** **Fluoride. Drinking Ourselves to Death?** - *Barry Groves , Newleaf ISBN 0-7171-3274-9*
*** **Porphyria. The Ultimate Cause of Chronic Disease** - *Stephen Rochlitz, PhD.*
    ISBN 978-0-945262-59-6

The visible and outward symptoms of Allergies and Food Intolerance are growing problems in our society and around the world. We should not however confuse them. They are two separate conditions but closely connected in the mind of the individual;

- **An allergy** is a condition where a person is sensitive or reactive to a particular commodity, sensitive to ingestion, even to the sight of the commodity, or he presence of the commodity.

- **Intolerance** on the other hand is much wider and for any food item it may be for a period, long or short or even permanently.

This is an area of healthcare where science and politics need to focus and invest in research. When they come up with explanations I believe it will include the role of and weight of additives and chemicals in our environment and food supply that has brought us to this point.

Medications were growing in popularity all through my lifetime. By the 1960s, the use of prescription medications was growing as was over-the-counter preparations for simpler or everyday complaints. I found that decade by decade, the use of both categories of medications was on the increase. Whilst many of those products had beneficial effects, they were nevertheless chemicals and all chemicals have side effects, many of them serious. Oestrogens were one such category of medication used in the contraceptive pills and hormone replacement therapy (HRT). It is only in the past ten (10) years or so that science has acknowledged oestrogen as a cancer risk.*

Heavy Metals such as mercury, lead arsenic and cadmium have all left a mark on human health and like chemicals impacted on DNA. Mercury was the most obvious and indeed the most toxic of all metals, probably the most toxic compound on earth. It is used in dental fillings (amalgam), and also in vaccines as a preservative. Mercury is also emitted into the environment from power plants and batteries. Most people who had a number of chronic complaints such as brain fatigue, low energy, lupus, digestive disorders, vaginal irritation, reduced fertility, emotional distress, lowered immunity and unexplained pain, invariably had mercury toxicity. Mercury was central to their health complaints. These complaints would have built up over time with many layers of medications along the way.

Resonance testing revealed people were mineral deficient, particularly in zinc and magnesium. Some would also show selenium deficiency. Clearly getting to the root cause was key to their return to health.

---

* **Breast cancer and hormone replacement therapy in the Million Women Study**
Million Women Study Collaborators Lancet 2003; 362:419-427

Immediate detoxification was not always possible as the body would be too weak so an aggravation had to be avoided. Sensitive selection and step by step detox was therefore important. Replenishment with essential foods and nutrients alongside was also important. Some animal fat in the diet, grass fed beef, bone broth, fish oils and/or olive oil might be needed. Zinc and magnesium would also be required in most cases. I found these nutrients could, at least initially be in homeopathic form as it is more easily absorbed. Homeopathic detoxification I found was the most effective method to get cleansing at cellular level rather than just organ or tissue level. For more information on mercury toxicity read Dr Stephen Bourne, Dental Mercury Toxicity and Bio-Regulatory Medicine.*

Lead is also a toxic compound which had been used in paints up until the '60s. The use of resonance testing would indicate metals in both tissue and cells, reflecting how children that chewed the top of their cot still carried the effects of the toxin in their system some thirty years later. Arsenic can be encountered in the environment, in the soil, water and air, so we are all exposed to it. Clearly it is our own responsibility to inform ourselves on these issues and take the necessary precautions.

I believe that metal toxicity has an adverse influence on the brain and brain function and unless it is addressed it will bring about neurodegenerative disorders such as Alzheimer's and dementia. I have no doubt that when science comes to understand brain disorders it will list heavy metals amongst the key causative factors. Scientists are already publishing on this topic and are pinpointing heavy metals as causative factors for brain function and disease. At this time Scientists recommend Glutathione as one of supplements which help in reducing the adverse impact as it binds with the toxic metals and helps remove then through the colon. **

Parasites cover a range of naturally-occurring bacterial, viral and fungal-type infections as well as worms, with which we have always been familiar. However, such pathogens are continually evolving and impacting heavily on our bodies. As living organisms, those parasites and infectious agents were responding to the effects of the toxic and pollutant materials mentioned in the foregoing paragraphs. They have always had a place to live and thrive with the human body as a host, but now they were competing within the body with unnatural compounds in the form of chemicals and metals which were from the parasites point of view, unwelcome intruders.

---

*   **Dental Mercury Toxicity and Bio-Regulatory Medicine** – *Dr Stephen Bourne*

** **Toxicity of Glutathione-Binding Metals** - *Federico Maria Rubino, toxics,*
    ISBN 2305-6304

** **Glutathione Is a Key Player in Metal-Induced Oxidative Stress Defenses** -
    Marijke Jozefczak, Tony Remans, Jaco Vangronsveld and Ann Cuypers toxics
    ISSN 2305-6304

Geopathic Stress was another issue which gave rise to health problems in people. Economic growth in the 60s had brought about a vast increase in house building and the same care was not given to planning as had been in previous generations. Houses were placed in locations to facilitate road frontage, traffic planning and so on, rather than the wellbeing of future inhabitants. Room location was not planned in such a way that people could sleep in a manner in which they would benefit from the natural characteristics of the planet. Simple advice would be to sleep with your head facing North. If there is a lay line found under your room the solution would be to move you bed to another location. If Geopathic Stress is a factor in your health it is best that you attend to it at first before you go down the road of other treatments.

Radiation is the outcome from electromagnetic frequencies that are emitted from power lines, radio, television and broadcasting apparatus, X Ray equipment and all electrical devices. The human body had become accustomed to and depended upon the normal planetary electromagnetic influences, such as the rays of the sun. These new electromagnetic waves generated by man through modern science now compete with universal electromagnetic influences which have brought about conflicts for man and animals. Whilst the world is dominated by electrical and electronic technology in our lifetime, I feel responsibility comes back to ourselves to minimise the impact of these stressors on us. If I have a concern for the future it stems from the impact of radioactive emissions on the health of the next generation, the children of the past decade who have had so much exposure to mobile telephones and other electronic devices. We really do not know what is in store because of the exposure levels. There is also the anti-social nature involved of continuous phone communication without the potential to interact and develop socially. I fear the emotional impact will be severe and will follow into physical health.

Deficiencies: how do they arise? Firstly, there was change in farming practices and in the manner in which food was grown. Fertilizers, how were the fertilizers prepared? Super-phosphates were widely used and presented as a means of enhancing crop growth and productivity. What impact had the increased phosphate have on the fertilizer mix? Did the addition of phosphorous (the super-phosphate) impact on the natural levels of magnesium and calcium in the soil? Did it alter the balance of minerals in the crops and did that alteration have an impact on the mineral content of the food? What did the scientific knowledge of the time tell us? Using resonance testing we could tell that many people were deficient in minerals, which we felt was a direct response to the change in farming practices which had disrupted traditional soil status.

Another cause of deficiency was the already stressed organs and cells as a result of any or perhaps all of the toxic compounds mentioned above. These toxins blocked absorption of nutrients from the food. The digestive system would normally utilise natural enzymes for the extraction and absorption of the essential nutrients before their distribution to organs and cells. As a result, cells were undernourished, organs became stressed and underperformed, body immunity declined and slowly chronic health conditions emerged.

Health Complaints

By 1974, I was now full time in practice. As you might expect clients were mostly from the home parish and surrounding parishes. Gradually practice expanded and within three years clients came from many counties. South city and county Dublin people were in the majority. Women accounted for about 96% in the first five years. Over the years, the proportion of male clients grew and in the last fifteen years the ratio has been 90/10, women to men approx. We need to make allowances here that women will also include children as Mom usually accompanies the child. What were the prominent health issues that I came in contact with? I will concentrate on the key recurring issues.

Candida, also referred to as *Candida albicans*, candidiasis or yeast infection. In conventional medicine, the yeast infection is the term normally used and as you might expect antibiotics are the standard prescription for these symptoms. What is candida. At its simplest it's a simple yeast, a natural mycotoxin that lives in the intestinal tract of every human, child and adult alike. You will have heard of baby thrush. It's the same yeast that causes the irritation to the baby. Clinically we refer to it as fungal, say it's a fungal infection. It is more acceptable for men that way as symptoms for men may be in the form of a slightly enlarged toe nail where a white lump has accumulated under the nail. Alternatively, it may show on a finger nail.

The question arises then, why does a natural mycotoxin cause such problems as has arisen and which has escalated to an international epidemic. The answer to that lies in the fact that we humans have altered the natural terrain in which this strain of yeast has lived throughout the millennia. We have altered the internal terrain, the internal micro environment which we call the digestive system. We have changed the inputs, we have altered the balance, we have added unnatural substances, we have disturbed the natural habitat and the eco system which has sustained this form of micro-life for millennia.

All life forms fight back, humans are not alone in that respect, so this yeast micro-life fights back for its survival and in the process, converts to a defensive, aggressive, predator, handing out many different health challenges to its host. Yeast overgrowth now has a clinical label, *Candida albicans,* a systemic pathogen.

Researchers have identified some of the many contributors to candida as poor diet, unsuitable foods, antibiotics, birth control pills, excess alcohol, heavy metals, mercury amalgam fillings and more. The yeast overgrowth thrives in the presence of refined sugars, refined carbohydrates, dairy products, processed foods, hormone secretions, and internal stressors like elevated cortisol. As the overgrowth continues to flourish, feeding on the excess sugars, the immune system continues to lose ground and the body becomes more sensitive as it struggles to protect itself. It will produce more mucous to shield the cells which in turn will give rise to other unpleasant symptoms, thus attracting further courses of medication, which in turn will damage more of the friendly bacteria and exacerbate the problems. The elimination system is under stress and fails to work adequately. Constipation is a feature and bowel movement is an effort. Everyday foods like milk and cheese, white floor and deserts become harder and harder to handle. The body is becoming more and more acidic. The once friendly micro-life has responded and has become an aggressor. The results for the host will be chronic health conditions such as, sinus problems, respiratory infections, inflammation, ear infections, premenstrual stress, acne, anxiety, fibroids, ongoing vaginal irritation, chronic fatigue and emotional distress. Following all of that you will have absence from work, reduction in productivity, lower income and lower quality of life. Worst of all I believe serious conditions are building for the future such as Alzheimers and dementia.

Candida was accompanied in many people with by other troublesome infections like Helicobacter Plyori (Hp), heavy metals and chemicals. Hp was not problem by itself but alongside other toxins it could be a specific issue. This combination of toxins in the gut expanded the difficult health issues to wider and physical health.

Digestive issues, have been studied for over 30 years by researchers looking at malfunction of the digestive tract in different ways and at different levels. We have a condition called Inflammatory Bowel Disease or IBD. This has three subsets:

- *Crohns Disease*, an inflammatory disease of the total digestive tract identified by Dr Burrell Crohns of New York. Pitting or inflammation can occur from the throat right down to the anus. This pitting or ulceration is a natural collection point for bacteria.

- *Ulcerative Colitis* or *UC* is an inflammatory disease of the bowel area, as opposed to the whole of the digestive tract.

- *Leaky Gut* is a condition where the gut has perforated and instead of the natural protection which it is supposed to provide, food, toxin, parasite or narcotics leak out, enter the blood stream distributing toxicity and spreading damage.

Digestive issues start with personal habits especially unhealthy eating habits. The fast pace of society in the past half century means people have lost time for many of the essentials of life. One of those is eating meals in an orderly and helpful way. We rush meals or eat on the move so we fail to get digestion going in the mouth. Food travels to the stomach where it meets with hydrochloric acid (HcL) and digestive enzymes. Here it is broken up and prepared for absorption and availability for the cells. When we rush the eating process, especially with heavy protein and dense foods there are failures in the system, due to inadequate levels of HcL. Some of the food will just sit and putrefy, or rot. The stomach can accommodate this for a time but eventually it will emerge as a problem. One outcome will be more gas and maybe foul smelling faeces, that is the down flow outcome. Another is the up flow outcome, where bad acids are produced, travel to the oesophagus where it shows as *acid reflux.* Antacids are prescribed for this, which like many medications adversely affect the natural flora balance in the digestive system.

HcL diminishes as life progresses so we must assist with replenishment. Take family meals at regular and appropriate time of day. Chew slowly, relax and enjoy the event. When digestive symptoms appear use celery juice as a daily cleanser. Eliminate, or at least reduce as much as possible sugars in the diet.
Dr Natasha Campbell McBride has published an excellent book which I recommend, on the connection between diet, the digestive system, gut health and mental and emotional health mental conditions, especially autism.*

Menopause was another of the troublesome issues for women who came to see me. They had the usual night sweats, hot flushes, fatigue, irritability, loss of energy, low libido and so on. One observation on this was in the early 70s such women were 50+ years. By the mid 90s I was having visits from much younger women, even as young as 35 years. HRT had been in use for 30 years by then. It was described as helpful by some, not so helpful by others. However, it was the side effects which were giving them grief, made worse by earlier use of birth control pills, medications, poor diet, non-active lifestyle, chemicals and heavy metals had all played a part.

---

* **Gut and Psychology Syndrome** - *Dr Natasha Cambell , Mc Bride Maidnform. Publishing. ISBN 0-99548520-2-8*

The downside was more difficult menopause and at a much earlier age. One other issue that I noted was the many nurses who came for help. During their training, indeed during their working years they had never been introduced to hormones or to the role or impact of hormones in the body. For those who had been recommended HRT, their doctor never explained the wider implication, only saying this will help with your symptoms.

The middle years of life should not be looked upon as difficult, rather it is a period in life when change takes place. Many women will recall an expression during the 1960s and later, *she is going through the change*. That was the menopause, but people did not use the word or refer to hormones. Probably most had never heard of hormones like oestrogen of progesterone. As we age oestrogen levels decline, but so also do progesterone levels. So balance is lost and discomfort is felt. The toxic load adds to the discomfort level.

I recommend that people stay with precautionary approach and use natural remedies as relieving measures. Use filtered water so as to minimise contamination. Take care with animal products especially meat and dairy. Use trusted organic sources to avoid antibiotic use or other hormone treatments. Do likewise with vegetables so as to avoid herbicides and pesticides. Cut out oestrogen mimics like synthetic cosmetics and toiletries.

Use Olive leaf to help with bacterial and viral infections, Wild yam and homeopathy to balance hormones and combine all with a healthy and balanced diet and adequate exercise.

Parasites feature regularly in health conditions. It is important to distinguish the status of the parasite such as:

- Is it the benign variety which is normal and at home in its host.
- Is it the visitor that has come to partake, picked up in a casual manner from a pet or maybe from a food.
- Is it a visitor that has got out of control, competes with the traditional parasite and is changing the ecosystem to its own liking.
- Are the nutrients that should go to the host been stolen by the invader. If so natural immunity and natural defences suffer further.

Those invader parasites however do perform a function. As many people have co-infections such as chemical and heavy metals, the parasites feed on those non-natural toxins and effectively are now part of the detoxification process.

The task for the Therapist is to determine which should be prioritised for elimination. For further reading on the subject, Dr Hulda Clark conducted extensive research on the impact that parasites had on the body and in particular their contribution to cancer*.

Viruses are another of the permanent features of the mammalian species. These viruses are under control when the body is in a healthy state but can develop a new strength when immunity and resistance is low. Another example of the importance of the immune system. The viral strains that tested most frequently were:

- Influenza virus which causes problems with the respiratory system and which is very transmissible by coughing and sneezing.
- Herpes Simplex causes cold sores and can also cause genital eruptions.
- Herpes Zoster, a more complex strain of herpes virus will cause fatigue, chicken pox, usually in children and shingles in older people.
- Epstein Barr (EBV) virus is a strain within the wider herpes category and is associated with glandular fever, chronic fatigue, fibromyalgia, certain forms of gastric and other cancers, strange taste in the mouth, skin eruptions, thyroid dysfunction and nervous system lymphomas.

Of the different viral strains, EBV is the most troublesome. It can lie dormant in several organs or gland such as liver, spleen and kidneys. It can spread to any organ or gland and seem to work in tandem with other co-infections including bacteria and chemical and heavy metal infections. A host of conditions follow like chronic fatigue, inflammation, lupus, thyroid problems, fibromyalgia, and tinnitus.

Occupational health brought many clients with a variety of complaints such as:

- Industrial workers and motor mechanics had reactions to lubricants like oil and grease.
- Farmers had lung complaints, respiratory problems and allergies to hay dust.
- Construction workers had asbestos poisoning and allergic reactions to various materials especially insulation materials.
- An airline pilot had reached the point where he had to give up work as his immune system was overwhelmed from the continuous radioactive impact of the cockpit. Radiation detox and nutritional rebuilding gave him an extra 10 years flying.

---

* **The Cure for all Cancers** - *Dr Hulda Clark PhD ND. New Century Press.*
ISBN 1-890035-00-9.

- Nursing and medical personal also felt the impact of radiation from working with high powered electrical and electronic devices.
- Highly computerised rooms with people working under pressure also gave rise to stress. In addition there was a higher than usual radiation content.
- Executive stress was at a very high level from extensive travel and continuous pressure for increased sales and profits.

Lifestyle and Dietary issues were a regular feature of a poor health condition and were a contributory factor in many of the other conditions mentioned. The desire for better income, a bigger house to a better location, expensive holidays or clothes all put pressure on the individual or family which show up in the quality of health. As a result, there may be insufficient time for home cooking, good quality food, family time, personal time, exercise, rest and reflection. Media presence expanded, belief systems changed, confusion levels grew and personal responsibilities were abandoned as populations were urged to demand increasing levels of services from government, from hospitals or from other sources. The levels of chronic illness essentially exploded.

The importance of a good diet was an issue throughout all the years of my practice. It was difficult to convince many of that. As an example, the connection with food and brain health was something people found hard to understand. The growing levels of processed foods now available from manufacturers together with the convenience associated with precooked foods make it attractive for consumers and so home cooking has declined. Education and training in schools has also declined or ceased altogether such that the present generation of decision makers are ill equipped to cope with the emergence of high levels of chronic illness. Processed foods and changes in farming practices are significant contributors to poor health. The levels of phosphate in the diet from land fertilising, food additives and processing is well catalogued by Herta Hafer in her book, where she places particular emphasis on excess phosphate contribution to learning difficulties and behavioural problems such as bad behaviour and juvenile delinquency. In healthcare language we use terms like ADD and ADHD.*

Children's Health came in a variety of conditions from extensive colic to autistic spectrum disorders. I found that mercury fillings and mercury from other sources was a big contributor to colicky babies who were poor feeders and had other digestive problems.

---

* **The Hidden Drug - Dietary Phosphate** - *Herta Hafer. Georg Thieme Verlag.*
  ISBN 0-646406-44-2

Mothers who breast fed passed their own toxicity to the infant, but I still recommend breast feeding. I am very much in favour of pre-pregnancy detox. Both parents should prepare in advance with up to one year for the mother-to-be. Get a full detox program, metals and chemicals and parallel that with a nutritional enhancement plan. Ensure you have an adequate level of essential minerals and vitamins.

Children with attention deficit disorders and autism-like behaviour tested for mercury poisoning which they had developed after weaning but also had other intolerances, particularly to gluten and dairy. Milk itself is presenting as a problem including an increased autism risk.*

Mineral deficiency was a regular contributor in cases of children and young adults who were poor feeders. Some with learning difficulties who also had relaxation and concentration problems. Detox combined with nutrition relieved many of these troubled cases. Vitamin D and magnesium deficiencies were most prominent.

Mineral deficiencies result from early birth as too early delivery can result in inadequate nutrient and essential bacteria transfer to the baby. Nature has established the 9-month gestation period which should be honoured. Caesarean sections should only be used when necessary i.e. when the baby is in breech. When the baby is born, if he/she is cold, a great place to put him/her is alongside the mother's thigh for warmth.

The effects of vaccinations on babies and young children can be detrimental. This needs to be examined scientifically as materials like mercury and aluminium are used as preservatives. Scientists have differed as to which of these are the culprit whilst other scientists insist vaccinations pose no risk. Other specialists hold the view that it is the combination of live viruses that is the culprit. Apart from the makeup, my own view is that the event itself and the childs health at the time of the vaccination is crucial. If the immune system is unable to take it the impact will be felt in brain cells.

This marks the child for life in so many cases. I believe the Health Authorities ought to review this aspect of public health, listening to the opinions of the best independent scientists available as well as the views of the parents. I think that heretofore they have been entirely reliant on the opinions of the pharmaceutical experts.

---

* **Milk - This traditional dietary staple is now a problem for many. What is science saying**
Martin Murray. Positive Health Online – Issue 226, November 2015

Fertility was also a recurring issue and troublesome for many. It is a modern lifestyle issue directly related to toxicity levels, nutritional status, hormonal issues, oestrogen levels in the body, emotional status and age of trying for pregnancy. Anxiety develops when early success in not achieved, so unless this is also addressed more difficulties arise. I found difficulties arising with both partners, each highly toxic and in some way nutritionally deficient. Sperm count was low in men due to mineral deficiency, particularly magnesium and potassium and the effects of electromagnetic stress was also present.

Body Acidity or pH, impaired balance was a recurring condition which was almost entirely due to the high proportion of acidic foods in modern diets. The acidity in turn led to a host of other conditions which showed up in the form of symptoms such as inflammation, gout, osteoarthritis and ultimately cancers. These conditions were treated with antibiotics, anti-inflammatories and painkillers all of which added to the acidic load.

The big contributors initially were refined sugar, wheat, dairy products, red meat, processed foods and fast foods containing of high levels of phosphates. This was at the expense of alkaline foods like green vegetables, cabbage, cauliflower, onion, broccoli, garlic or spinach. Education on dietary matters is the key to resolving these problems. Dr Robert O Young produced a very valuable and easy to use book on body pH, which gives plenty of advice on the role of food in health.*

Addictions was an issue that increased decade by decade. In the 1970 it was largely alcohol. It was mostly wives that came for advice. How could they cope, husband was great otherwise but the drink made him a demon. Marriage break-ups or separations were not socially acceptable back then. As the years went on alcohol continued but gambling also came into the picture. Later a new emergence was illegal drugs. In newspapers it was a city only problem, but that was incorrect, the problem was spreading. Mothers were distraught. By the end of the 1980s there were new concerns. It was spouse or parent concerned about addiction to prescription drugs. I well recall an appointment made by professional gentleman, he was concerned about his wife. This lady also a professional was mid 50s and she was on 15 different drugs per day. These drugs were prescribed by four different consultants. His calculation was that she had visits to at least seven consultants in the previous 4 years. So three consultants had not prescribed and one had suggested she should cut back on the medications and he recommended she see a counsellor. Her husband supported that approach but she resisted it. He felt that the consultant visits gave her a feeling of status but in his view it was an addiction.

---

* **The pH Balance** - *Dr Robert O Young and Shelly Young. Piatkus Books UK.*
  ISBN 9 78074939816

This type of addiction grew steadily and continues today. Private health insurance facilitates it but it is still an unnecessary drain on resources. Some people don't want to heal.

Adrenal fatigue, was a problem for many people. I would say that six out of every ten women of menopausal age had low adrenal function which added to their feelings of fatigue, lack of vitality, low libido levels and increased stress levels. I also found teenagers were adrenally fatigued. It is a reflection of the fast pace, must achieve, highly stressed society of our time. The adrenal glands are two small pea sized glands that sit like a bishop's cap on top of each kidney. With the pituitary, pineal and pancreas they are an integrated part of the wider endocrine system thereby influencing several important body functions like hormone production, fertility, libido and sexual health. The adrenals produce a key hormone, *adrenaline*, which is an energy booster, a communicator which acts spontaneously when the body needs help. As an example, if you are walking in the countryside and ramble into a field where you then find there is a Bull in amongst the cattle. You get startled, maybe frightened. The Bull may be timid, maybe not, but automatic instincts are to get out of that field to the safety of another. It is the adrenals that have gone into action, produced an adrenaline rush and advised the correct course of action.

However, in our fast-paced society there are constant demands on our time, with deadlines and commitments continually having to be met. Most days an adrenaline punch is called for. When the adrenal glands have excessive demands they get fatigued and cannot produce adequate levels of key hormone, *adrenaline*, which impacts on the CNS, (central nervous system), resulting in brain fatigue. There is then the knock on effect and production of hormones like oestrogen, progesterone and testosterone are slowed down resulting in lower energy and low libido. Healthy adrenals are very important to a healthy pancreas and healthy thyroid also. Indeed they go hand in glove. A healthy pancreas is essential for the production of *insulin*, a natural hormone to regulate the use of blood glucose. In addition the adrenal glands assist the thyroid gland to produce adequate thyroid hormone.

Hormones are essential to life as without them we would be lifeless. They are tiny messengers of a chemical nature which enables the various organs and glands communicate with each other and so enable the various glands and organs perform their natural functions.

Adrenal deficiency can come from a variety of influences, excessive stress levels, toxins in the body, allergies or reactions to basic foods like coffee, sugar, dairy or beef.

Difficulty sleeping was a key issue in for many people with adrenal fatigue. People take supplements believing they are health giving but they may be reactive to an individual supplement which will cause stress. Same applies to medications or indeed the filler in the tablet or capsule.

Thyroid function and in particular underactive thyroid was a very common problem for people. In conventional medicine this would be referred to as *goitre*. I found a strong relationship between toxins in the body, viral infection especially EBV and adrenal and nutritional deficiency all of which resulted in low thyroid function and inadequate thyroid hormone production.

Stress was another recurring issue. However, it was the follow-on effects which gave rise to serious issues like heart disease and cancers. A certain level of stress is essential, it keeps us active and motivated. However, when it becomes chronic or routine it is clear something needs to change. It can be employment or business, social or personal life relationship or lifestyle. If stress is not managed or controlled, it will result sooner or later in so many other difficulties. Anger will follow, bad behaviour will result, employment potential and social connections will decline. We need to educate people in the importance of self-care and early intervention. Simple exercises like Emotional Freedom Techniques (EFT) can relieve or help manage stressful situations. Yoga, meditation and appropriate exercise are very important. All of these are no, or low-cost health protectors. With experience, natural remedies like herbs and homeopathy can help further.

Weight and Obesity. In the early years, it was excess weight that concerned people but in the last decade the word "obesity" is used more frequently. Over the four decades, like every other therapist, I have seen the increase in the waste lines and it was a gradual increase in BMI, or body mass index. Now it is recognised and indeed acknowledged by medical experts that obesity is at least as a precursor to disease, particularly cancer. However, we are well aware that long before now that it is a contributor to diabetes type 2, elevated blood pressure, high cholesterol, heart conditions and more.

Obesity, like many of the conditions already mentioned have common causes, such as lifestyle, inadequate exercise, city living, a food supply high in sugar, fat and salt, and environmental toxins. But it is not as simple as dieting or following a programme for a number of weeks. Dr Heli Good has presented a very precise picture on the internal biological mechanisms which are triggered and activated in the cycle that leads to BMI level which would have a person classified as obese.*

---

* **Obesity, a modern, mismanaged, and misunderstood malady** - *Dr Heli Goode. Positive Health Online, Issue 232, Aug 2106.*

Three (3) hormones play a key role in the process, **Leptin, Insulin** and **Ghrelan**. For people caught up in the dilemma of obesity and the Practitioners who guide them it is important to understand the role of those hormones.

Fat that is stored produces hormones the most important of which is leptin which works on the brain particularly the Hypothalmus. This is an important gland within the Limbic System from which the overall hormonal network is managed. The leptin hormone is the information system that tells the body it is in need of food or has sufficient for its needs. However, when yo-yo dieting, a programmed approach, or environmental **Obesogens** enter the system, the body's natural control system is over ruled and control is lost. Obesogens are environmental toxins that mimic the body's own hormones and throw natural regulation off course.

Insulin is a hormone produced in the pancreas which has the role of utilising sugar and the distribution of it to the cells for energy or for storing. When disruption in insulin production takes place, the fat is stored rather than convert- ed. One of the downsides of this is the development of diabetes type 2 with its many consequences. High levels of insulin have many downsides like the onset of arthritis, inflammation, skin conditions and infections.

Ghrelin on the other hand is the hunger hormone which informs the brain that the body is hungry and needs food. When ghrelin is disrupted, again the wrong signals may be sent to the brain and imbalance results by continuing to take in food that is not necessary.

Any health programme addressing the issue of body mass or obesity needs to address the role the brain plays as well as the emotional impact on the individual.

Low immunity was a very common complaint and there was no surprise in that. When you look through the range of complaints listed above you will find that many are exacerbated by an underactive natural immune system. This is a critically important element in human biology. We are created by nature to be self-supporting and that includes self-healing. However when we are frequent- ly or persistently engaged in activities including unsuitable diet or lifestyle we compromise or overload our innate immune system. Take for example if we are sensitive to sugar or white flour but continue to have those commodities in our diet we will eventually suppress natural immunity and leave us vulnerable to other conditions. The same principle will apply to other toxins in our body or stress overload to name a few causes.

Unlike other organs such as the liver, heart or bone the immune system cannot be seen, touched, moved or operated on surgically. Nevertheless it is crucial to our wellbeing. The principal associated glands and body systems are the Thymus, Spleen, Blood, Lymph and Connective Tissue. All of these interact and work in harmony and in turn connect with the Endocrine and Nervous Systems to provide optimal biological function from which good health follows. The thymus is a source of life energy, the spleen is a filter system for the blood, the blood is the source of life for every organ it nourishes, the lymph drains the waste from the system and the connective tissue is the transport system which carries and distributes nutrients to all parts of the body. Keeping all those organs and glands in a healthy state is vitally important.

Mental Distress has been a key issue in my practice from the start but its significance has grown dramatically in the past ten years. Reasons for these distressing conditions vary from person to person but in general I found that a common cause tied into the same wider issue of diet, lifestyle, occupation, toxicity, medications, life experiences, relationships, childhood traumas and hereditary factors. These can be summarised as follows:

• *Anxiety*, a natural part of human makeup, is necessary to some degree as it keeps us focused, helps us set targets and work towards objectives. However, it can hurt us if we are the worrying type, overly ambitious, and fail to recognise the wider picture of our society.

• *Diet* was poor quality which gave rise to digestive disorders, such as Crohns and IBS, infections such as Candida. Regular courses of antibiotics were prescribed which had little beneficial effect but over time gave rise to various side effects including loss of hope and resultant anger.

• *Food Sensitivity*, with gluten, white flour and sugar collectively or individually as key components in depleting the Immune System and having a knock-on effect as sensitivity to other foods arose. Milk and dairy products were also common triggers for many.

• *Toxicity* came from food additives, such as colour and taste enhancers all of which are chemicals. Other chemicals such as herbicides, pesticides and heavy metals, particularly mercury are detrimental to healthy brain function.

• *Relationships*, mostly between spouses but also parent-child, sibling-sibling, neighbours and work colleagues. Residual effects of relationships with parents, siblings, teachers, headmasters or other authoritarian figure of the past continued to have negative effects on people twenty or thirty years later.

- **_Loneliness_** came up many times and it was most evident in people who from a distance had everything going for them. Many were professional or white-collar workers. They were married with families. Parents put all available time into family and lost connection with family of origin. As jobs changed contacts were lost and over time communication skills were lost. Loneliness set in and emotional wellbeing declined.

- **_Modern living_** brings its own stressors, childcare, mortgage repayments, household bills, unemployment, social conditions and many other issues.

- **_Medication_** and the medical system has an enormous impact on people's wellbeing for good and ill. A visit to a GP can result in a prescription. It was accepted as necessary or essential. Recurring visits brought more drugs. For many the problems got worse, Consultant visits followed and maybe hospitalisations. Many found the experiences difficult and others found them stressing to one degree or another. Trust was lost and mental anguish set in.

- **_Inherited influences_**, known as **_miasms_**,* either with or without personal experiences give rise to many problems which cause lower quality of life with many physical health issues resulting. These include destructive emotions such as anger, hate, fear, distrust, envy, greed, jealousy, confusion, ingratitude and more. I came across so many people carrying such a heavy load with many years lost in the prime and middle years. It was mostly women in the 30s to 60s age bracket with some of them carrying issues into their 70s. As examples they hated the husband, didn't know exactly why, he is a good man. Next would emerge the stored hatred for his mother, maybe a sister, then another sibling. Sometimes it was the doctor who didn't cure them, the drugs that made them ill. On it went, the neighbour that would not talk but talked to every other neighbour.

- Some people held grudges for teachers they did not like, seeing the teacher as not liking them and singling them out for particular punishment or exclusion. Some of the memories were very direct experiences, while others were childhood memories of a parent beaten by a teacher or otherwise victimised by a Priest, Landlord or Civil Servant.

- Some people held **_memories_** of violence in the home, father beating mother or another sibling. Treats of violence or punishment featured, you will be sent to the Industrial School, was an example.

---

* _Miasm comes from the Greek " miainein" meaning taint or pollution. It was brought into moderm medical vocabularly by the founder of homeopathy Dr Samuel Hahnemann when he referred to conditions to which people were predisposed. In effect he was referring to negative inheritances such as family and/or societal prejudices which contribute to illness for the individual._

- **Low self-esteem** was an ongoing issue for people, some mild but very deep in others. Much of this resulted from childhood experiences which had never been overcome, despite in many cases the individual person having "done very well" in adult life, with a successful marriage, family, progressive lifestyle maybe even a successful business. Low self-esteem is a particular lifetime burden for so many, hiding it, managing it, fighting it, submitting to it or using it in so many ways, to avoid a school play, social outing or family get together. People take on the most negative interpretation of routine happenings, see themselves as part of it, see shame or guilt in it and interpret it as directed at themselves. Not all negativity results from family but also from other sources including wider society as local tradition and historical convention can play a part. Through their own actions people troubled in this way self-sabotage regularly and set themselves on the path to exclusion and loneliness. They reach a state where they are able to say hi or good morning or other minor exchanges but are unable to have a conversation or communicate, particularly at soul or spirit level. Their internal grievance about some issue, real or imagined is brought forward and allowed to dominate their day. The ongoing isolation that follows is as toxic to wellbeing as any of the chemical nasties the environment can throw at us. Failure to get advice, failure to take advice, refusal to learn, is all part of the agony. However in the wider context, we must accept it is all part of the learning process and individual lifetime journey.

- The underlying problem was the personal level of **distress** which had been stored. This was expressed as anger and hate against various parties whether family, neighbours or wider society. In these cases, the sources and triggers must be identified and cleared so that healing can begin. Otherwise the problems are perpetuated and passed to the next generation where the negative feelings are displayed in irrational thinking and bad behaviour. I found in some cases it was adopted by observation by the younger whilst in other cases by wilful action by the senior. In many cases it was passed upward by adult children to elderly parents. So many of these cases always thought, some even insist, that right was on their side, they personally had the authentic view of how life should be.

- **Words** can be healing, words can be wounding, so we have to be careful with our words and how we use them. Thoughts can be healing, thoughts can be wounding, so we need to be careful with our thoughts. Our words express our thoughts so it is so important to be balanced and grounded in our thoughts.

The subconscious mind

The subconscious mind is so powerful. This is the mind that stores everything, all events in our lives, good and bad. Unfortunately, it is the bad that is recalled so frequently and the negative influences that flow can severely disrupt the quality of life for both the individual and the people he/she loves.

Kinesiology is such a great tool as it enables you to communicate with the subconscious mind as a means of helping people unravel their internal confusion. Natural therapies, particularly homeopathy are very good to connect energetically and help restore balance. It is a process, time is required, trust is required, the practitioner can guide, the client also has to participate if progress is to be made. Many of the people I met and treated were deep down genuine loving people and great parents or friends. However, some event or events in early life or in the womb had been recorded in the subconscious which held them back or in some cases prevented them from learning and growing. Louise Hay provides a very good book on the connection between destructive emotions and physical illness.*

Forgiveness will have to be a key part in any therapeutic plan for recovery. Forgiveness of the offences and the persecutor alike. Self-forgiveness must also be part of the recovery plan for in the end we are responsible for our own lives and how we live. Bearing grudges is a toxic process, it will eventually eat into our being and damage quality of life. Words can be healing, words can be wounding, so we have to be careful with our words and how we use them. Thoughts can be healing, thoughts can be wounding, so we need to be careful with our thoughts. Our words express our thoughts so it is so important to be balanced and grounded. In the heat of an argument or debate, in the course of a marriage, a business, a school term things are said which cannot be unsaid. But they can be forgiven, they need to be forgiven because lingering hurts remain on both sides. Therefore it takes two, they must reciprocate and heal. Colin Tipping has produced an excellent book, *Radical Forgiveness*, which comes with a work book on how to prepare for, operate and manage forgiveness. **

I should emphasise that whilst inheritance aspects are very important, the individual's own personal development also plays a role. Some examples I witnessed was personal behaviour during the boom years up to the financial crash of 2008. Certain people were progressing in life as business was booming. Builders became hoteliers, developers became magnates, musicians became celebrities and so on. Many others wanted to be like those stars. Greed was at work fuelling other emotions such as envy and jealousy.

---

* **Heal Your Body** - *Louise Hay. Hay UK, Astley House, 33 Notting Hill Gate, London W11 3JQ*
** **Radical Forgiveness** - *Colin Tipping*, *Colin Tipping Global 13 Publications, ISBN 978-0-9704814-1/2*

Grounding was lost, balance went astray and with loss of control, anger, hate and fear follow. I find in the past 20 years that anger is so prevalent in society. I do not recall anything like that in the years up the 1980s, it has grown dramatically in the past 30 years. We all have to reflect on why our society is so troubled and what can we do individually to rebalance it.

Multiple issues, apart from above there were people with many of those conditions in combination. The medical term would be co-morbidities. People would have had diagnosis for migraine, for shingles, neuropathy, chicken pox, frozen shoulder, Bells Palsey and in recent years Lyme disease was added. Many were desperate and it was entirely understandable. No wonder emotional distress is at epidemic proportions and growing. That is why we need holistic healthcare, where we look at the person, the whole person and not just at the current symptoms he/she suffers from. Every person who comes in will need the full kinesiology or bio-resonance assessment for the range of toxins, infections and parasites as well as the nutritional deficiencies and emotional status.

The therapist or practitioner has a key role to play. Every client is an individual, we are all different, have different needs have had different experiences. Some have learned from their experiences, some are in the process, some are struggling with the learning process. Our role as healers is to try and understand, to be compassionate, to be with them. We cannot take on their problems but our empathy with them is part of the recovery process. People are soul searching, they are looking to their souls to get some signal that they are on the right path. Are they currently doing what their soul was guiding them towards and how are they doing in the process.

Limbic Health

In the restoration of emotional wellness, treatment or regeneration of the limbic system will be very important. The word limbic means, *border* in Latin, describing the border structures around the basal regions of the cerebrum. This region of the brain is home to many important glands including the hypothalamus and the hippocampus. The hippocampus is the area that deals with memory so it will need attention when attending people needs as mentioned in the last paragraph. It will also need attention when dealing with memory loss and it many difficulties associated with aging. The hypothalamus plays a key role in brain function as it directs the communication pathways within the limbic. Several aspects of the endocrine system like emotions, behaviour, hunger, thirst, body temperature and water regulation are all associated with different parts of hypothalamus.

Therefore, treatment of the limbic system and associated glands will need specific attention. Additionally, the pituitary and adrenal glands which form part of the endocrine system would need support as part of overall emotional health restoration.

Emotional issues arose in the clinic many times over the years. Memories come up, tears flow, pain is released and so on. The source can be varied from childhood, to school, sibling rivalry, adolescence or abuses in the work place. Whatever the source it is healing people need. It is a challenge for the therapist. I use kinesiology, homeopathy and flower therapy. I also recommend yoga, prayer, meditation and exercise. I would talk to clients about their belief systems, their practices, motivations, aspirations and so on. I found a strong relationship between desire to achieve, which included status, celebrity, material and wealth accumulation, with loss of personal identity and connection with roots. Many people had lost their spiritual connection and direction also. Faith in its traditional meaning had been set aside as many people now placed their faith in their current happenings and the new environment. Difficulties had now arisen in their lifestyle and some of the old hurts were brought back.

In so many of those cases I felt their individual souls were calling, connecting to the body and mind and sending signals in the form emotional distress, which progressed to physical health. In such cases, meditation and/or prayer is an essential part of restoration of balance. Of course, it can be traditional prayer and reflection such as was practiced up to 30 years ago. However, the strict and rigid control of the Church in itself had some negative impact and was a source of stress to many. More choice is available now. It can also be the addressed through new approaches such as meditation, yoga and mindfulness all of which assist and guide personal reflection. Whilst these practices may be new in our society in western countries, they have been in use for thousands of years in eastern countries. In health, science and spirit can work well together.

Chapter Four

Home Remedies

Home Remedies

Acne (facial) a home remedy for acne is to boil buttermilk until thickened. Add pure, raw honey so that it becomes a thick cream. When cool, apply to the affected area of the face or shoulders.

Acne/Boils, take a small pinch of sulphur every day and mix with butter. Apply to boils or acne. Another option is to press used Echinacea tea bags on the acne or boils for 5 minutes.

Adrenal function is essential to good health. Healthy adrenals are key to healthy thyroid and pancreas function as they enable essential hormone production. Good adrenal function is helped by regular meals, not to heavy, with an appropriate in between snack such as an apple, fruit bar or protein bar.

Good foods for adrenal health are asparagus, sprouts, broccoli, lettuce, kale, blueberries, blackberries and raspberries. Homeopathy is very helpful. Herbs include Ginseng, Rhodiola and Astragulus. Chromium and magnesium are important minerals.

Alcoholism, take 1 teaspoon of chromium and vanadium mixed together twice daily. This will reduce the desire for alcohol. Sucking on a whole Clove will help to stop craving for nicotine and alcohol.

Allergies, an allergy is a common and almost continuous occurrence in society at this time. If the body detects a foreign substance like a metal or chemical or pollen, it is described as an allergy. Some refer to it as hay fever. Even the smell of fresh cut grass can trigger a reaction. The symptoms are runny noses, sore or itching eyes, burning in the lungs. Take wild plum bark syrup, peeling of orange skin mixed with boiling water and drink it as a tea. A spoon of honey is also useful. Drink a glass of water every hour and do this for a few days.

Alzheimers, another of the emerging health tragedies of our time. In effect it is the traditional senile dementia of the past with a new label. I believe it is very much a direct result of modern living, lifestyle, the food chain, excess sugar intake, blood sugar levels, the effects of diabetes, chemicals and heavy metal toxins including mercury.

Prevention is the best solution through a good and healthy diet which nourishes your gut. Support that with suitable supplements and detoxify regularly to minimise the effect of metals and chemicals. So I recommend you:

- Avoid pathogens such as moulds in home and food supply.
- Avoid exposure to parasites as certain parasites travel to the brain.
- Be careful to address inflammatory conditions including foods that cause inflammation.
- Heavy metals should be avoided including mercury, lead, and cadmium. Use regular detoxification procedures to lessen the adverse effects.
- Minimise grain levels in your diet and avoid gluten as much as possible.
- Minimise dairy in your diet as much as possible.
- Avoid processed foods and maximise wholefoods in your diet.
- Use good fats such as olive oil, nuts, seeds and avocados.
- Include adequate levels of greens and leafy fresh vegetables in your daily meals.
- Eat oily fish such as salmon, mackerel, herrings and sardines. Avoid the bigger fish such as tuna as it may carry toxins. Use wild caught fish as farmed fish can be treated with chemicals so as to look like the natural product.
- Include in your diet, beef, lamb or chicken but search out for grass fed or organically raised animals so as to avoid chemicals including antibiotic residues.
- Include coloured berries in your diet particularly blueberries, strawberries and raspberries. Use organic produce fresh in season and preserved or frozen out of season.
- Use supplements to support brain health including B Vitamins, (including B12) Omega 3 Oils, either fish or plant, but ensure they have the correct ratio of omega 3 to 6. Magnesium and Selenium are also important as essential minerals.
- Add coriander to your diet or take in supplement form as it is good for heavy metal detox.
- Herbs such as Rhodiola, Skullcap and Ashwagandha are good for brain health.
- Homeopathy is very good for brain health but you may need resonance testing to identify remedies specific to your needs.
- Avoid stress as much as possible and take corrective action where it is a constant issue, such as stressful employment, social or familial difficulties.
- Good sleep is important so practice a routine which enables you to obtain 8 hours per night.
- Exercise regularly (ideally daily) for both body, mind and spirit, in a manner that suits your body strength, personality and outlook.

, a certain level of anxiety has merits as it helps us build and grow. y is intensified due to mineral deficiency such as chromium and magnesi- thyme tea twice daily can be helpful. Homeopathy and Flower therapy are both very effective.

Arthritis, falls into two forms, **Osteo and Rheumatoid.**

• **Osteo,** is closely associated with lifestyle and diet. For large joints, such as hip and knee, the use of those joints will play a part. If you are an active and/ or competitive sports person you will have wear and tear to cope with. This will increase your exposure to osteo arthritis which will intensify as you age. However diet plays a huge part. An acidic diet will impact on cartilage which will gradually wear away until bone connects with bone. Inflammation adds to the discomfort and pain. To minimise impact eliminate acidic food from the diet as much as possible. Rub olive oil on effected joint for two to three minutes, leave for another two minutes and wipe clean. Deficiency of nutrients contribute in particular calcium and vitamin D.

• **Rheumatoid,** is a condition categorised in medicine as auto-immune disease. This is where the human immune system attacks one or more organs believing it is providing protection from an invader which is attacking the body. What if it is a traditional invader such as a virus or parasite. I have found people with ongoing joint pains, sore bones and inflammation where viral infection, mostly EBV and parasites are present. The chemical and metals toxins can also be present. In can even be the metal toxins, particularly mercury that gives rise to the inflamma- tion. Natural remedies including homeopathy and herbs for the Nervous System and Immune System are important in the battle against this condition. Use olive oil topically as for osteoarthritis as pain reliever. Olive oil in the diet will also be helpful as will blueberries, ginger and green tea. Use curcumin to relieve the inflammation, homeopathy to treat the virus or parasite infection. Nettle leaf is a helpful herb and sulphur (MSM) is good for joint recovery.

Asthma, the use of breathing exercises that change the balance of oxygen and carbon dioxide in your body could help you control symptoms such as tight chest, wheezing and shortness of breath.

Lemon juice in water is helpful. Honey is soothing. Thyme is a good anti-inflam- matory and it can help to reduce spasms in your airways to prevent an attack. Gingko Biloba can also help and studies have found that taking a daily supple- ment could improve your peak flow. However, Ginko is a prescription herb in Ireland.

Athlete's Foot, a fungal infection which can result from continuous use of rubber-based footwear. Rub the inside of the toes with a black banana skin to the affected area. You can also apply some crushed garlic with Vitamin E. Alternatively apply garlic directly. Mix tea tree oil with juice of garlic and apply. You may need homeopathic treatment if the fungus is deep rooted.

Autism, another of the modern health conditions of our time and a tragedy for the children who will be the adults of the future. Like other conditions referred to in this book, I strongly believe it is almost wholly connected with modern day living and the environment in which we live. This of course is the toxic environment into which babies are born and in which women live whilst baby is in the womb. So even before birth babies have life obstacles placed in their way. Heavy metal toxins are to the fore here with specific emphasis on mercury. There are numerous published articles at this time which point to mercury as a causative factor. I agree with that but it is not alone, we also have vaccines which were preserved in mercury or aluminium and we have an array of chemicals from cosmetics to household cleaners and furnishings. Diet can also be a factor and milk, the food most revered food for children has emerged as a potential cause.

Home treatment of autism offers the best options for better quality of life and as near as possible to a normal life. Pharma medications has shown to be little help and may indeed add to the toxic load. Identification of the individual toxins is the first step and cleansing the system of those invaders. Homeopathy is the best treatment I have found, with a selection of Xenobiotics which are homeopathic preparations of individual toxins, be it a metal, chemical, medication or food such as gluten. Using kinesiology your practitioner will be able to identify which toxins are a problem and the order in which they should be drawn out. In the same manner, a suitable diet can be drawn up geared towards minimising symptoms and restoring emotional stability. Help for parents and siblings can also be identified using the same identification path. In addition to the homeopathic treatment, supplements will be important especially Vit C and Omega 3. Dr Tinus Smits studied autism extensively and said *don't despair.* He combined homeopathy and nutrition as a treatment modality which he named Cease Therapy.*

Bacterial Infection, you can make your own home antibiotic.
<u>Ingredients</u> are : 4 Onions,
4 Cloves of Garlic,
½ Pound of Dark Brown Sugar,
Juice of 4/5 Lemons,
1 Pound of Honey.

---

* **Autism Beyond Despair, Cease Therapy** - *Dr Tinus Smits M.D. Emryss Publishers, March 2010*
ISBN/EAN: 978-90-76189-28-4

Method: Place all ingredients in a delph or glass bowl, place a tea cloth over the bowl and allow ingredients to ferment for 4 days. Drain the liquid from bowl into glass bottle or small jar. Dosage, Adult 6 drops, 2-3 times per day when infection is present. Child, 3 drops, 2-3 times per day. In cases of severe and unknown cause or if symptoms persist you should obtain professional advice.

Bedwetters, this is often an emotional problem. Diet: no salt and no fat. Avoid all colourings and preservatives. Give pearl barley water every morning as a remedy for kidney and bladder. Put the crown of the head facing north when sleeping. Put orange colour on the right-hand side of the body and have them looking at indigo blue or violet. Give the child a hot bath before going to bed. I also suggest plenty of outdoor exercise is helpful. For example, take him/her for a walk and get him/her to breathe deeply to stimulate the circulation and this will also help to overcome the emotions that have been a basic part of the problem. Encourage children to eat fresh and dried fruit such as bananas, grapes, plums and apricots. Drink plenty of water and avoid drinks that are high in sugar. No fluid after 6 pm. Rub St John's Wort Oil over the child's bladder when in bed.

Bleeding gums and broken capillaries. Wash and cut 6 lemons (organic where possible) into small pieces. Cover with two pints of water and bring to the boil. Turn off the heat and let sit for 25 mins, stand and set aside until cool. Take 6ozs twice daily for ten days. In case of bleeding gums, hold juice in the mouth for a while.

Blood Health, to decongest your blood, the following recipes have worked well for many. Take 4 onions and cut them into pieces, add to water and simmer to make onion water. White and red onions together have more anti-clotting properties. Drink ½ cup of onion water 4 times daily. Take 500mg vitamin B6 with each cup of onion water. Do this for 2 days in a row. One clove of uncooked garlic daily is also a good blood thinner. Pick a healthy diet – tomatoes, rice, millet, bananas but continue with vitamin B6.

One teaspoon of sheep sorrel added to a mug of boiling water is a good blood cleanser. Rosemary is known as a blood thinner and it helps the circulation. To improve blood circulation, put ground red pepper in your socks. The vitamin A in carrots is a good blood support. Red beetroot is also good for the blood. Bananas contain potassium, which we need to keep the blood healthy. Hawthorn and Echinacea are good blood cleansers for blood poisoning. Wear indigo coloured garments as your intention of attaining good blood quality.

Blood Pressure, is directly connected with adrenal gland stress especially adrenal insufficiency, so adrenal support is essential. Potassium helps to control high blood pressure as does Mistletoe and Angelica. Mix one teaspoon of each in one pint of water. Bring to the boil and drink 2 cups per day. Garlic also regulates blood pressure. It can be used for low blood pressure and high blood pressure and it can prevent stroke. It helps to unclog arteries coated with plaque. Potassium from fruit and vegetables such as peas and beans are helpful. The homeopathic remedy for high blood pressure is Uranium Nitcum. For low blood pressure it will depend on the causative factor but could be Gelsenium or Nat Mur.

Body Odour, to combat body odour, drink tomato juice daily. Parsley also prevents body odour. Use a liver cleanse frequently. Further aids to combating body odour are Zinc, Calcium, Magnesium and lots of green vegetables in the diet, including alfalfa.

Boils, garden Sage and Cornmeal as a poultice works well. You can also use a Flaxseed poultice. Crush Epsom salts and glycerine, mix together to a stiff paste and use as a poultice.

Bowels, to sooth the bowels, simmer flaxseed for about 20 minutes and leave to stand for about 1 hour. Then put 3 tablespoons into 3 cups of boiling water. Let it boil down to half, add a little sugar to taste, then add the juice of 1 lemon. Drink it all at bedtime. It is excellent to take once a week. Flaxseed helps to prevent cramping of the bowel. Tea made from Cinnamon Bark taken 3 times daily will heal a bleeding bowel. Black Pepper as a tea will help a running bowel. Alfalfa seeds help make the bowel move. Always check for worms.

Brain Health, I believe brain function is directly related to the quality of water and food. Water contaminated with pesticides and heavy metals is very damaging and in time I believe science will make the link between those toxins and condition such as memory loss and Alzheimers. Apart from food, avoid heavy metals like gold or silver on the person.

On the food side avoid wheat where possible. Oat is a very good brain food. Suitable animal fats are important as the brain is largely fatty tissue. Sage on a slice of Rye Bread works well for the brain. Coconut is also a good brain food; you can cook with it or take it on its own. Eyebright tablets help to strengthen the memory. Cardoon, a plant in the Artichoke family is good for the brain. Mustard seed improves memory. There are many homeopathic combination remedies which improve brain health.

Bronchial and Lung problems, use a brown or white paper bag, squeeze the bag, put it over your mouth and breathe in and out for about 5 minutes. Do this many times a day. Thyme tea every hour is also good. Take Dandelion tea and Fennel about 4 times a day. For mucous conditions, add cloves and honey as this will relieve nausea and vomiting. Always take Echinacea 4 times daily.

Bruises, Iron Phosphate will help. Traumaide is a very effective homeopathic cream.

Burns and Scalds, place the burned hand or area in ice water or cold water until the pain is gone. If it is a second or third degree burn and no physician is available, mix in your blender ½ cup wheat germ oil and Vitamin E and ½ cup of honey. It is a detoxifier. When the oil has dried out, put on a Comfrey compress. Comfrey leaves encourage cell regeneration. It helps new, clean cells grow in a jiffy. Pick fresh Comfrey leaves but do not wash. Put the leaves straight on the wound and a bandage to keep in place. Change the leaves every few hours.

Aloe Vera applied to burns will help with healing. Egg whites slightly beaten and applied to first and second degree burns promote healing. For minor burns, run under cold water for several minutes. For serious burns call for medical help.

Calluses and Corns, soak feet in hot water for 5 minutes. Tape Lemon slices and Castor oil to the corn or callus every night. Rub peppermint oil on callus to promote healing.

Cancer

I consider this to be a disease of our time, part of our essence and being; *our within and without*. This degenerative disorder has always been with us. However, within the last fifty years, its prevalence has risen dramatically. Statistics indicate that both incidences and constancy will continue to emerge. How do we account for it? I believe it has a strong connection with modern farming practices, including excess fertilisation of land and changing food processing procedures. Lifestyle practices, diet, occupation, stress and excessive levels of medications are also contributing factors. Look no further than your water or nutrient sources as two key influences which may help minimise risk of toxicity to your cells. Factory produced chickens are fed antibiotics 36 days out of their 39-day life. Think about that. Antibiotics are used throughout the food producing sector. The most common medication for cows is used to treat mastitis. Antibiotics are also used as growth promoters. Percy Weston, an Australian farmer and Naturopath came to the conclusion that excessive phosphorous in our food supply was a key contributor to cancer.

He conducted experiments on his own farm with sheep. When the land was fertilised with superphosphates, the sheep developed arthritis symptoms at first and cancer followed later. When he moved the sheep back to organic grass, the arthritic symptoms would clear up in about three or four weeks.*

The pace of modern living, unsuitable personal ambitions, uncontrolled ego and psychological conflicts all combine to disturb and unbalance healthy emotions, creating conflict and derailing inner harmony. This makes our bodies more vulnerable to chronic diseases. Viral infections, including the Epstein-Barr Virus, increases our risk of ill health, especially within the reproductive organs. I believe prevention is the first step in helping limit and control serious diseases within the coming fifty years. I also recommend *'Your life is in your Hands'* by Professor Jane Plant, as essential reading for anyone wishing to start protecting their health. **

The role of diet has long been a bone of contention when it comes to chronic disease. In the 1940s, the medical profession maintained that scientific evidence available gave no indication that nutrition was of specific value in the control of cancer. Now there are many studies which correlate poor diets with cases of cancer. There is also sufficient evidence to suggest a diet containing fresh, organic and seasonal fruits and vegetables can help reduce the risk of some cancers.***

Unlike other conditions where simple home remedies can be applied, cancer is a multi-sourced, multi-dimensional illness of the whole person. It therefore requires a multi-dimensional approach to its prevention and treatment. Professional help will always be required and I strongly believe in a broad-based strategy, combining the best of traditional and complementary medicines as well as modern scientific medicines.

Modern medicines such as chemotherapy and radiation need to be managed by specialist personnel such as oncologists and doctors, whilst naturopaths, kinesiologists and homeopaths will provide guidance on the traditional and complementary segments. However, real responsibility will rest with oneself. An article by my colleague Ronnie Plant is very informative - *'You are what you eat, drink, sleep, believe and practice'*. It's a blueprint for living, which I recommend.****

---

* **Cancer, Cause and Cure** - *Percy Weston. Bookbin Publishing. ISBN 0-9758137-0-6*
** **Your Life in Your Hands** - *Prof Jane Plant Virgin Publishing Ltd ISBN 0 7535 0850 8*
*** **Cancer and Common Sense** - *Dr Douglas Brodie, Winning Publications ISBN: 1-884367-03-8*
**** **Healthy Aging** - *Ronnie Plant, www.nhacademy.eu*

In addition to the information provided in Chapters 4, 5 and 6, you could consider the following as additional measures, alongside conventional treatments:

- **Clean water** in the home is essential. Install an undersink filter that will remove up to 90% of the contaminants including fluoride, chlorine and heavy metals.
- **Eat only** grass-fed beef or lamb and source organic if possible.
- **Include** free range and organic chicken.
- **Leafy green** and other vegetables such as broccoli, cauliflower, spinach and cabbage as all have anti-tumour properties.
- **Lycopene**, an active phytochemical found in tomatoes, is good for prostate tumour progression.
- **Curcumin,** a major component in turmeric, offers wonderful antioxidant and antiangiogenic properties.*
- **Green Tea** can be consumed as a tea or taken in supplement form as Green Tea Extract. It has known benefits for breast and prostate cancers.**
- **Milk Thistle** is an important herb as silymarin, the active ingredient, is considered an anti-metastatic compound.**
- **Vitamin D** deficiency will raise risk of breast and prostate cancers.***
- **Vitamin E,** in particular its gamma tocopherol compound, provides protective properties against certain cancers.**
- **Omega 3 Fatty Acids** from fish is an important element in the prevention of many types of cancer.****
- **Oestrogenic foods** and medications should be avoided due to their oestrogen-mimicking substances. Also consider cosmetics and household products and their toxic potential. *****
- **Acidic-forming foods** should be avoided or reduced from your diet where possible. This includes beef, pork and dairy products. Preferably, it is best to seek Practitioner guidance on this.

---

   *   **After Cancer Care** - *Gerald M. Lemole, Pallav K. Mehta, Dwight L. McKee, Rodale Publications, ISBN:978-1-62336-502-8*

  ** **Thrive, don't just survive** – *Dr Geo Espinosa. Riverdale Publishers. ISBN 9 781517 287325*

 *** **After Cancer Care** - *Gerald M. Lemole, Pallav K. Mehta, Dwight L. McKee, Rodale Publications, ISBN:978-1-62336-502-8*

**** **Fatty fish and fish omega-3 fatty acid intakes decrease the breast cancer risk** *BMC Cancer 2009, 9:216 doi:10.1186/1471-2407-9-216*

***** **The China Study** – *T. Colin Campbell, Thomas M. Campbell, Benbella Books Inc, ISBN: 978-1932100-66-2.*

- **Homeopathy** is a safe and effective therapy, which may be integrated with conventional treatments as well as alongside acupuncture and other comple mentary modalities. This can also help alleviate side effects of chemotherapy, radiotherapy and hormone therapy.*
- **Acupuncture** helps relieve pain and promotes relaxation.
- **A positive lifestyle** should include suitable and regular physical and emo-tional activities. This includes cardio exercises, meditation, yoga and prayer.

Candida, this is now a significant problem for many people. Diet is a major contributor as are medications and heavy metals, especially mercury, so you will need professional advice to work out a new health protection plan. Individuality is important and food commodities that effect one person may have no effect on another but may seriously impact the third person. As a guideline the following will minimise your risk of candidiasis by avoiding the following:

- Sugar and high sugar foods like honey, maple syrup and quick acting carbohydrates.
- Bread and bread products containing yeast.
- Alcoholic beverages including beers.
- Sauces and vinegar containing foods. Use fresh lemon juice instead of vinegar.
- Processed and smoked meats like salamis and sausages.
- Cheese products, including Swiss and cottage cheese. Mould varieties are highest risk.
- Dried and sweetened fruits, melons and fruit juices unless juice is freshly prepared.
- Edible fungi like mushrooms and truffles.
- Nuts such as peanut usually contain mould.
- Vitamins and mineral products unless marked "yeast free".
- Leftovers in fridge as they may contain mould.

As a home help you could try a magnet under the right foot, it may give relief. Taking 1 teaspoon of Vinegar in water every morning can also help. If the can-dida infection has already built up to a chronic level you will need professional detoxification at cellular level.

---

* **Cancer and Homeopathy** - *Dr Jean-Lionel Bagot. Unimedica, Narayana Verlang Nlumenplatz 2 D-79400 Kandern Germany. ISBN 978-3-944125-21-3*

Chest Problems, fill blue glass bottle with water. Place in the sun for 15 hours and then use as a drink.

Chilblains, mix ½ lb of washing soda in a basin of hot water, steep affected area in water for 20 minutes each night for 7 days. The same water can be retained but must be boiled each night.

Cholesterol, to lower Cholesterol exercise for 20 minutes twice daily. Cut out all animal fats. Eat lean grilled meat and fish, use low-fat dairy products, no more than 1 egg per day. Eat plenty of green vegetables and fruit. Eat wholemeal bread, brown rice, wholemeal pasta and breakfast cereals of bran, oat bran and porridge.

Chronic Fatigue, another of the conditions of the modern era which can include headache, dizziness and chest pains in many cases. I found that both bacterial and viral infections will be present as well as heavy metals. All combine to wear down the sufferer who will most probably have had medications along the way. My experience was that medications will not help but diet and suitable supplements will.

To restore health have any pathogens identified and detoxified. Include in your diet fresh vegetables like sprouts, asparagus, celery and spinach, cucumber, kale and garlic. Include berries, especially blueberry, apricot and grapefruit. Suitable herbs are Lemon balm, Nettle and Red clover. Zinc and Selenium are important minerals and Curcumin helps with inflammation and support for the CNS.

Colour, all colours relate to organs in body, wear one colour and look at another, important to wear colour on right hand side of body, Red is connected to the base and crown chakra, orange associated with the stomach area. Yellow is emotions, adrenals and pancreas. Green is the heart. Blue colours aid throat and chest area. Indigo and violet are for the head chakra. Pink is calming.

All black suits and outfits are very fashionable but I recommend some colour every day. It can be a blouse and shoes to match your suit, a colourful scarf or a simple band on the elbow or wrist.

source: iStock.com/bert_phantana

Common Cold. The common cold has been with us forever. Science has spent hundreds of millions trying to understand it and find a cure through pharmaceutical drugs. Maybe they have given up by now. I look at the cold as a routine part of the workings of the natural immune system, the body's way of managing itself. From time to time it will indicate that it needs to cleanse and detox. It activates its defence mechanism and sets about clearance. I think it is best to rest for a few days, take hot lemon drinks and plenty of other fluids. Do not try to kill the cold with alcohol or drugs.

Connective tissue, is a very important part of our of our biological and structural system which has an impact on the whole body. In physical terms it connects cells, in cartilage it is flexible whereas in bone it is hard and inflexible. It is made up of special proteins or glue like substance which act as binding or connections between cells and carries out functions like hormonal messaging between blood vessels and cells. A key function is to distribute nutrients. However it can become clogged if toxins enter the system and remain there, it is important that drainage is provided through the lymph.

Lymph massage can be very useful and homeopathic detoxification is also important for healthy connective tissue.

Constipation, is more than a discomfort to people. It can cause serious complaints when toxic waste accumulates and contaminates the blood, which is then distributed to other parts of the body causing inflammation. Examples could be sore knees, joints or painful shoulders. Practice experience suggests that:

- Dehydration accounts for one third of all cases. To resolve this, drink at least one litre of clean water per day.
- Unsuitable foods accounts for another third. Eat healthy foods and get resonance testing as needed.
- The final third could be due to other issues such as emotional concerns, anxiety or even depression, for which professional help is required.

Cough, to make remedy you will need 6 organic eggs and 6 lemons. Put lemon juice over eggs in shells in a glass dish, cover with cloth and leave in fridge for 48 hours. If you want to preserve, add some light brown sugar and 2 tablespoons of brandy but don't add this if it's for children. Remove the eggs after 48 hours and remove from the shells. Beat eggs, lemon juice, sugar and brandy well and keep in fridge

Cramp, carry a bottle cork in trouser pocket and place under pillow at night. Muscle cramps could arise due to magnesium deficiency.

Cystic Fibrosis, a condition brought on through gene inheritance which as a result sufferers need special diet and attention. To get started;

- Avoid potatoes, tomatoes, aubergines, peppers, lettuce, chillies. Avoid selenium, a mineral found in water and soil and also be wary of foods grown in soil-rich selenium.
- Avoid cocoa, chocolate and all foods and drinks containing cocoa and all sugars for 2 years, after that use only brown sugar.
- Avoid fruits, particularly strawberry, cherry, rhubarb, kiwi, gooseberry, plum, appricot for 2 years. After that use only apple, peach, nectarine, raspberry, blackberry, blackcurrant and cranberry.
- Avoid vegetable such as veg marrow, endives (chicory) mushrooms, seaveg, such as dilisk and carrageen moss, also radish, walnut and wheat germ.
- Acceptable vegetables are beetroot, peas, parsnip, sweetcorn, sweet pepper, tomato.

Cysts, are lumps that form under the skin and are described as epidermal or sebaceous. The latter are usually associated with a hair follicle. Cysts are normally not malignant and many will clear up by themselves. They can be hard and lumpy but some will fill with pus or liquid. If a cyst is troublesome you could make a poultice of washing soda moistened with ethylene glycol, not too runny. Apply daily for about seven days. When cyst softens such that it is ready for eruption, a fresh cabbage patch cover for a few hours will usually draw out the pus. The wound will clear up within a few weeks.

Ovarian cysts are another type of cyst known as polycystic ovarian cyst or PCOS syndrome. This can be unpleasant with fatigue as an ongoing feature. Check for viral infection as EBV may be a factor or parasites may be present. Homeopathy is very effective and can avoid the need for surgical removal.

Dairy, products can be troublesome to many people especially those who are lactose sensitive. If you are sensitive avoid cheese and yoghurt products. Use soya or coconut milk instead.

Food Additive Sensitivity, is a problem for many people. Avoid processed foods which have chemical additives such colouring, bleach or MSG (monosodium glutamate). Over the last decade spelt flower has become available again so I recommended it. If you can't find spelt, use plain white flour without additives. Use wholemeal pasta. Make your tea from loose tea leaves as tea bags are bleached. Boil drinking water if you don't have a kitchen filter.

Dandruff, boil a handful of Willow leaves. Strain and wash your hair and scalp in it, three times a week for two weeks.

Dehydration, was very common amongst clients over all my 45 years of practice. People are simply unaware of the importance of water on a continuous basis. The human body is approx 70% water with different organs varying in composition. So we need continuous replenishment, with at least one litre per day for adults and half for children up to 12 years.

An effective way to receive your water requirement with added benefit is to boil 4 sticks of celery in 4 litres of water. Bring to the boil, simmer gently for one hour, allow to cool, refrigerate and you have a 4 day supply.

Detoxification, essential in the modern world. Detailed procedures are outlined in pages 86 - 88.

Diabetes, has become more and more prevalent in the last 25 years and like other health conditions is a precursor for other serious illnesses. There are two categories of diabetes known as Type 1 and Type 2. Diabetes Type 1 is also referred to diabetes mellitus. It arises when the pancreas is unable to produce Insulin or adequate levels of Insulin to regulate sugar levels in the blood. Insulin is a hormone produced in the pancreas which is produced as the sugar levels rise immediately on receipt of food into the digestive system. It controls the level of sugar in the blood so that it does not raise to excessive levels. When blood sugar rises to a high level or excessive level it is referred to as *hyperglycemia.* When it drops to excessively low levels it is known as *hypoglycemia.* Both excesses levels must be avoided.

Hypoglycemia will produce symptoms such as dry mouth, loss of taste, unnecessary hunger, fatigue, difficulties with vision or urination. Why the pancreas is unable to produce adequate levels of insulin is not precisely known by scientists. However we must firstly understand that the pancreas must itself be healthy so infections from virus, bacteria, or environmental toxins will certainly play a part. Dense and protein rich food can be a problem if there is too much intake at once. Christmas time would be an example, with mixed meats, rich cakes, plum pudding, mince pies and cheese all combine and could overwhelm the pancreas.

Type 2 diabetes can effectively be controlled by diet and life style. Avoid foods as much as possible which are high in sugar and fat, especially saturated fats. Be careful on portion sizes, keep to what is appropriate to your energy needs and spread intake over your three daily meals, maintain a healthy body weight and exercise regularly and appropriately.

Include in your diet spinach, celery, kale, asparagus and sprouts. Also blueberries and raspberries. Fenugreek is a good herb for the pancreas. Take zinc and chromium, magnesium and silica supplements. Omega 3 and Vitamin D will also support the pancreas.

Diet, to achieve a perfect diet you only need to obey 6 basic rules:

- Be sure to eat a balanced diet.
- Select foods that are low in saturated fat.
- Select foods that are low in sugar.
- Select foods that are high in fibre.
- Eat meals regularly at suitable times.
- Relax during meal and eat slowly.

source: iStock.com/Elenathewise

Ear Ache, onion juice can be used as ear drops - 2 drops in the ear to reduce infection. Alternatively put 2 drops on cotton wool and insert gently in the affected ear. Homeopathic Ear Sensory is also very good for unexplained ear ache including children's aches.

Ear Wax, can be a problem for many. Ear candling is very effective as it will soften and run out the wax. Take care with the type of candle as some brands are not as effective as others. Another solution is Olive oil. Heat a spoon, place 3 drops of olive oil on the spoon and tilt it into the ear whilst holding the head sideways.

Earthing, and connection with the earth is very important for good health. Due to the move from the land and more city living, people have lost contact with the earth and lost the benefit of earth energies. This loss of earth energy and the prevalence of electricity as energy has produced stresses for the body which causes inflammation and adds to existing adverse health issues. The best

approach is to get out into the country side frequently, walk barefoot on the green grass as often as possible. If you are a city resident you can get earthing shoes for walking and work and earthing mats to use at your work station. For home you can place an earthing blanket over your mattress. For more information on the role of earthing read Clinton Ober and Dr Stephen Sinatra*

---

* **Earthing. The most important discovery ever?** *Clinton Ober, Stephen T. Sinatra ,M.D., Martin Zucker. Basic Health Publications, Inc ISBN 978-1-591209283-7*

Electromagnetic stress, comes from mobile phones, radio and TV and the many electrical devices in the kitchen and home. I think the most troublesome of these is the mobile phone because of the continuous use and especially by children and young adults. Avoid wearing the phone on your person. Keep the phone away from infants and babies. If breast feeding do not feed your baby with the phone at your side.

Emotional health, varies greatly from person to person. Often times a calm exterior hides turmoil inside which many people do not know how to handle. It can be home, work, society, inheritance, childhood or a multitude of reasons. Stay calm as much as possible with each new challenge, sleep on it for a night or two, avoid rushing in. Think and say nice things to yourself, about yourself, about others. Say some nice things about others to others. Work on trust in yourself first, then in your partner, then others. You will find there are friends, you will find there is help. See health, general below.

Endometriosis, is a condition that causes inflammation, period pain, infertility and may lead to ovarian cancer. Excess estrogen is a contributor as are mycotoxins and chemical toxins. Keep the body warm, use hot water bottle when pain is at its worst. Detoxification is essential and suitable nutrition when trying for pregnancy.

Excess Electricity, use steel comb to comb back the hair against its normal lie which will draw out excess electricity from the body. Also, you can hold it against the palm of the hand to activate adrenal function and against the fingertips for overall release.

Eye Health, for sight maintenance,

- Juice ½ potato, ½ onion, ¼ green pepper and drink 8ozs of this a half hour before your supper for thirty days and watch your eyes getting clearer.
- An infusion of dried camomile herbs, cooled and soaked on to a couple of cotton wool pads, can help to relieve itchy eyes. Put pads on eyes and leave on for 10-15 minutes.
- Slices of cucumber can also revitalize eyes in seconds.
- For sore eyes or conjunctivitis, use a wash or compress of fennel, camomile or marigold tea, well strained and with a little salt added. Soak in cotton wool and put on eyes for 15 minutes, 3 times daily.
- Fennel and marigold have a reputation for strengthening the eyesight. Apply a little onion juice to sties. Be careful not to get it in to the eye.

Eye Health, for sight improvement there are 3 essentials:

- **Manganese**, if you are having trouble seeing at a distance you may need up to 210 milligrams of manganese daily. This mineral must be absorbed in salt form, Manganese Gluconate is recommended. Purpose is to improve elasticity in the eye.

- **Vitamin A** is good for eyes only when there is dim night vision. For main tenance of eyes, take 10,000 – 25,000 units of Vitamin A per day. For dim night vision take 50,000 units per day. If for example you cannot see blinking red lights on aerials at night, then you need vitamin A.

- **Suitable exercise**, is essential for good eye health. Darkness is very good for the eyes. Even with the eyes closed light penetrates the eyelids. Palming is an exercise I recommend:

Remove the glasses

Placing the palms of the hands against the surround of the eyes without pressing on the eye.
Palm the eyes with eyelids closed.
Look up as far as your eyes will go until it hurts, stretching the eye muscle.
Immediately return eyes to central position.
Move eyes to the right until it hurts.
Return to central position.
Move eyes downwards until it hurts.
Return to central position.
Move eyes to left until it hurts.
Return eyes to central position.
You have now completed a cycle.
Repeat cycle 10 times.

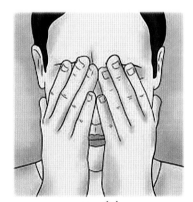

source: pt.wikihow.com

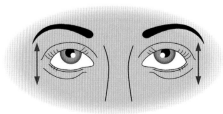
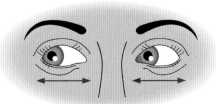

source: alldaychemist.com

These exercises will strengthen the eye muscles so as to develop the ability to shorten or lengthen the eyeball at will.

1)
- Hold a pen at arm's length.
- Focus eyes on tip of pen.
- Very slowly bring pen towards eyes, all the time focusing on the tip of the pen.
- On touching the nose with the tip of the pen, slowly return it to arm's length, still focusing on the tip of the pen.
- Repeat the whole exercise 10 times.
- If the object is blurred, don't worry, strengthening the muscle is the important objective.

2)
- For this exercise, lock the head in position and only move the eyes.
- Hold pen at arm's length.
- Move pen upwards until you lose sight of it, then return to central position.
- Move pen to the right until it disappears, moving only the eyes and return to central position.
- Repeat downwards and to the left.
- Always follow the tip of the pen focusing on the end point.
- Repeat the cycle 10 times.

3)
- This time lock the head <u>and the eyes</u>.
- Stand 6 feet from a wall and focus on the spot.
- Repeat all 3 exercises above.
- You focus on the spot on the wall but yet you follow the path of the pen.
- Purpose - to improve peripheral vision.
- Repeat cycle 10 times.

For Nearsighted People

As well as doing the exercises above the following will help:

1)
- Place the back of two fingers up to eyes alongside the nose.
- Walk around the room for 5 minutes.
- You will not be able to see straight ahead.
- This forces you to see out of the corners of your eyes.
- You will soon get flashes of the whole scene around you.

2)
- Get a 36 inch piece of string; tie 3 knots 6 inches apart.
- Tie one end to a chair or door knob and hold the other close to the nose.
- Concentrate on the first knot.
- The string in front of the nose will look like two strings coming together at the first knot.
- The string just after the knot should look double, getting wider as it leaves the knot.
- Some people are so near-sighted that the string will appear to come together in front of the knot.
- Concentrate on the 1st knot for a while then concentrate on the 2nd knot and finally on the 3rd knot.

Fibromyalgia, another of the modern health conditions which shows up as unexplained pain in the face, shoulders, arms, legs, in tissue with soreness when touched. Continuous fatigue will also be present. I found that there usually was viral infection, mostly EBV with chemical and heavy metals alongside.

Home solutions will include diet and supplements. Use fresh vegetables like sprouts, asparagus, celery and spinach, cucumber, kale, lettuce, garlic and ginger. Include berries, especially blueberry, apricot and grapefruit. Suitable herbs are Lemon balm, Nettle and Red clover. Vitamin B Complex is helpful in relieving the emotional stress and Zinc and Selenium are important minerals. Curcumin helps with inflammation and support for the CNS.

Gallbladder, people who cannot tolerate fat will need treatment. As a remedy you will need: 1 grapefruit, 1 lemon and 2 cloves of garlic. Peel and remove the stones. Blend it all together and take twice daily. Fresh lemon juice in a cup of hot water taken first thing in the morning will empty your gallbladder and start the day on a happier note.

Gallstones, to reduce risk and prevent stones forming take one tablespoon of ivy tea after each meal. To eliminate gallstones;

Day 1 - Eat cooked and raw vegetables only, drink plenty of water.

Day 2 - Vegetable juice only, mix well with saliva before swallowing. If you are juicing your own veg, refrigerate and drink within 2 hours. Drink plenty of water. In the evening take 2 ozs (or 2 teaspoons) of pure olive oil. Follow with a taste of lemon to kill the taste. Repeat the olive oil procedure 6 times at 15 minute intervals.

Day 3 - Stones should pass.

Geopathic Stress, is the term used for the adverse effects on the body of influences from the earth such as underground waterways and sub-terrain activity. These can be natural water courses, pools, caves, streams or they can result from manmade activity such as mining, foundations for tall buildings, sewers and drains. Geopathic energies are given off and can occur in homes, and workplaces with long term health problems for susceptible people.

Gout, the condition which results from "good living", too much wine with dinner and aperitif beforehand. An acidic body follows, especially uric acid. Cut down on the good life and eliminate high sugar foods. Celery as a vegetable is good as is celery water as a drink. Cabbage in the diet will be helpful. Sodium phosphate is very beneficial as is Omega 3 fatty acids.

Haemorrhoids, also known as piles can be very painful. Food rich in fibre is important as constipation is a key contributor. Carry chestnuts, one on each side of body. They can also be carried in pockets.

Hair, adding tea tree oil to shampoo helps with haircare problems such as dandruff and head-lice. Vinegar hair rinse keeps the scalp healthy and the hair conditioned. Dilute 1 tablespoon of herbal vinegar with 8ozs of water. Rub thoroughly into the hair and scalp. Leave for 5 minutes then rinse off. Parsley can also be good for dandruff. Use the following in the final rinse:

- Sage to darken hair.
- Chamomile or lemon to lighten it.
- Rosemary to condition dry, thin or hair that is falling out.

Hair loss, can reflect deficiency of essential amino acids. Use the south side of a magnet on back of hair brush which can help. As well, Silica and Horsetail (also rich in Silica) can improve hair growth.

Headaches. Dehydration (insufficient water in the body) is a major cause of headaches. Magnesium deficiency can also be a contributor. Foods containing lots of water are helpful in the diet such as watermelon, berries, cucumber, melon, tomatoes, grapefruit, apricots, peaches and cherries.
To reduce a severe headache, stir a teaspoon of honey in a glass of warm water and sip. In case of severe headache your body may be calling out for calcium. Take fat-free yoghurt, which is a great source of calcium and also ¼ teaspoon of ground egg shells. Dry the eggshells in a low oven to sterilize; this will take one hour. Keep a watchful eye so they will not burn, as they become useless then. Ground them finely when they are entirely cooled. Also, drink two glasses of fresh watermelon juice while your headache lasts.

Heavy metals toxicity, can be minimised with useful herbs such as Sweet sumac, Uva ursi, and Goldenseal root. Place herbs in cider vinegar and leave to stand in a warm place for 12 hours. Remove to a cold place and let it stand for a further 12 hours, strain and use, 1 tablespoon four times daily. Dulse and other sea vegetables are good detoxifiers. Parsley and Sage are good so spread on a salad. Garlic is another good chelator, so eat one raw clove per day. Homeopathy detoxifies at cellular level which is important for heavy metals. Treat the liver as removal of metals is stressful on the liver.

Health- Education, must ideally start in childhood at home and be continued throughout the school years. Bring your four and five-year olds to the table and have them help and participate in the baking and cooking.

Don't worry about spillage or a messy table as it will easily clean up. Let the child stir the mix and roll a few scones, make his/her own and place them in the oven. Motivation starts there. Teach them the importance of good food for good health.

I recommend that the importance of healthy eating and healthy food be a formal part of the educational curriculum. Hopefully the politicians will see the sense in this some day. Education should be about preparation for life not just about scoring high points to get into a profession or trade which may eventually not be suitable for the student who puts all their energy into pursuing it.

Health – General
Eat plenty of green vegetables – raw or cooked lightly in little water, organic where possible and preferably locally grown for optimum freshness. Avoid table salt including foods which are pre-salted. Chew food thoroughly. Eat only one meal with meat per day and try one day per week without meat. Avoid or greatly reduce intake of dairy products. Include roughage in your diet such as wholemeal brown bread, porridge and salads. Avoid smoking and excessive alcohol. Breathe deeply in fresh air. Exercise daily but within personal capacity, say a brisk one mile walk.

Health – Spiritual. Take time for yourself every day, maybe 10 minutes twice a day. Say some prayers or meditate whichever is your preference. Listen to soothing music. Go for a walk. When you build up confidence join a club, a gym, or yoga centre or help with your local Church or School. Do something helpful or positive every morning like letting a pedestrian cross the street or letting another driver into the line of traffic. Talk to a neighbour whenever possible but don't intrude. Think nice thoughts about yourself. Think in a positive manner about yourself. Think positively about something a family member has done for you. Call some family member or friend from time to time.

Do a favour for a neighbour or friend and don't look for thanks all the time. Tell somebody you love them when you feel like it. If you hold a position of responsibility such as a professional or a business don't overcharge unnecessarily. Like physical health, this is not a complete program, but it is a start.

High blood pressure, You will need 3 oranges and 3 lemons. Cut into pieces, boil in 2 pints of water for 15 minutes then add 2 tablespoons of honey. Boil for another 10 minutes. Strain and drink 6ozs three times a day before meals. In cases of diabetes this remedy should be avoided.

Hormonal Problems, colour therapy is useful in maintaining hormonal balance. Wearing orange or yellow can help or eating yellow food can help with menopausal problems such as hot flushes.

Hormonal stress is compounded by toxins from foods, chemicals and heavy metals. Herbs and homeopathy are very good for hormonal stress brought on by toxins and medications as well as for the adrenal fatigue that goes with hormonal distress.

Hospitalisation, can be an anxious time for people. It can also be risky as people can be subject to infections which they would not come across at home. If your hospital stay is planned take precautionary measures such as boosting your immune system in the weeks before your hospitalisation. Use homeopathy, herbs or nutrients which will boost immunity and prevent infections. Beta glucans or Zinc might be useful. Bring your own remedy to the hospital as an alternative to antibiotics which you will be offered. The same would apply to sleeping aids if you are taking anything at home to help with sleep.

House Health, can be improved by selective use of suitable indoor plants such as Fern, Aloe Vera, Cactus, Bonsai, African violet. You can build a mix of plants in a collection tray. Plants clean the air which is good for health, they give out oxygen, which we need and they absorb carbon-di-oxide which we exhale as waste. I recommend a selection of colours and variations for different rooms. Use the details in Chapter 7 on colour to decorate you house and have family health as a key element in choosing.

House Stress, can have an adverse effect on people's health if the immune system is unable to cope. Fatigue, frequent colds, irritability will be amongst the early symptoms. To minimize the effect, do not leave Microwave plugged in all the time. Avoid a Stereo beside the bed or too many electrical devices in the Bedroom. Avoid a split-bed or bed with drawers underneath.

Cats are a good indicator of a stress line as they will lie on it. Housed sheep that remain restless at night is an indicator of a stress line.

Immunity, is crucial to good health so maintain and support a healthy immune system. A healthy and balanced diet combined with adequate intake of clean water every day is the starting point. Get adequate and suitable exercise ideally every day. Reduce or avoid stress, combined with rest, recreation and relaxation are also important. Give time to meditation and or prayer. Do good works for yourself and others.

Add garlic and ginger to your diet. Supplements such as Vit D, Vit C and Magnesium are important for immunity.

Inflammation, is a recurring issue that is not well understood. It is part of the immune response, the body's natural inbuilt mechanism to protect initially and then repair at cellular level. Inflammation increase the blood supply, both red and white cells to the damaged or effected area. This may result in redness, swelling and heat. Mobility may be curtailed such as in damage to a joint. Rest is important as it permits the inflammatory process to bring about healing. The use of anti-inflammatory medications or painkillers can be avoided with good management of the condition.

Infertility, can result from several factors such as mineral deficiency, especially magnesium, toxicity in the body, over acidic body, excess oestrogen which may come directly from birth control pills or from the water supply. A healthy and suitable diet, the avoidance of zeno-estrogens (chemicals that mimic oestrogens) and restoration of mineral balance are good starting points. Fatigued adrenals are a frequent cause of sleeping difficulties so have your adrenals checked.

Insect Bites, mix bread soda and cream of tartar in a small amount of water, and apply paste to the skin.

Insomnia, a glass of milk with 2 teaspoons of honey will help make you sleepy. A cup of chamomile tea before going to bed and it will help to make you sleep. Another option is 3 drops of chamomile essential oil on a tissue and place it under your pillow or add six drops of essential chamomile oil to your bath.

Joint Pains, plaster a whole nutmeg on troubled joints for relief. Use bone broth with onion, maybe celery added, at least once a week. Use either lamb, fish, ox-tail or chicken. A kinesiology test will prioritise what is best in individual cases. For chicken use free range and for lamb or beef use grass fed. Fresh sea fish has the added advantage of iodine. Beef bone especially oxtail will need to simmer for two hours after bringing to the boil.

In cases of stiffness or soreness in small joints of the finger, either yourself or your partner press hard on the quick (base of finger nail) for 20 to 30 seconds. The pressure causes blood to flow after release which will help the joint. Repeat a few times a day. Where stiffness and soreness arises in toes stand on the ball of your feet with pressure on the toes. Support yourself with hands above your head on the wall. Circulation will improve after the exercise.

Kidney Stones, buy a 6 pack of Coca-Cola and 4ozs of pureed asparagus. Open the cans of coke and allow gas to escape. Consume the above within a 2-hour period. (I attribute this remedy to Rita Corley)

Kidneys also hold onto sludge when urination is slow or intermittent. Drink one cup of Birch leaf tea every day for a week. Then intermittently as required.

Leg Pain in Adults, can arise from inadequate calcium and inability to me lise it. Ensure you have sufficient magnesium so as to enable uptake of calcium. Excess phosphate in the diet inhibits calcium uptake. Leg pain is also associated with cadmium or thallium toxicity. Cadmium may come from water where galvanized pipes are used and may cause blocked vessels to spasm. Smoking increases the risk. Thallium toxicity can come from dental fillings.

Leg Pain in Children, is usually caused by mineral deficiency and /or presence of cadmium or lead.

Liver Cleansing Tonic, use the freshly squeezed juice of ½ lemon, freshly squeezed juice of ½ red grapefruit plus 2 tablespoons of virgin olive oil. Mix together and drink first thing every morning for 5 days. This combination can also be taken to dissolve gallstones.

Lyme disease, is a relatively new condition that has emerged in the past 25 years. It carries many of the symptoms associated with viral, chemical and metal toxicity mentioned elsewhere but with more intensity. It is named after the town of Old Lyme in the USA where it was first identified as an infection from a tick which carried the infection from deer. Since then it has fallen under the parasitic label. Proof of this source has remained controversial in both conventional medicine and natural therapies alike. Along the way other bacterial infections have been identified as co-infections. Most people will carry several symptoms such as chronic fatigue, muscular pain, joint pain, twitching, restless leg, brain fog all tied in to emotional stress and a feeling of helplessness.

American author, Anthony William describes Lyme symptoms as viral and rules out specific parasite or bacterium as an originating factor. Mr William attributes Lyme to a combination of many of the conditions of resulting from modern lifestyle and the environment including agricultural chemicals, mercury poisoning, fungal infection from molds, insecticides, excess use of medications, stress, personal trauma and existing low immunity.* Identification of the toxic and infectious compounds will be necessary and kinesiology is the best method that I am aware of. Detoxification will be needed for the causative factors and I found homeopathy essential for this. Useful herbs are Lemon balm, Thyme and Licorice root and Bladderwack. Zinc and Curcumin are important for inflammation and pain relief.

Lymphatic Drainage. Blocked Lymphatics show in the Groin and Ankle area. Take a hot bath and while still warm massage the body. Skin Brush upwards on the legs and arms (for a child you can use a nail brush). Also, brush the Kidney and Adrenals area.

---

* **Medical Medium** - *Anthony William. Hay House ISBN 978-1-78180-536-7*

Memory, dried apple peelings made into a tea are full of silicon and will help to strengthen brain function. Almonds are a good brain tonic, ½ teaspoon of Almond Oil daily will improve the memory. To improve concentration, take 1 Vitamin B12 and 1 Folic Acid per day. Herbs which provide comfort are Gota Kola and Rosemary taken every morning, Homeopathy is also very helpful.

For children's brain function use Dill and Alfalfa seeds are both beneficial. Clove in tea helps memory function.

Menstruation, difficulties arise for a number of reasons including viral infection, adrenal insufficiency, or diet with excessive levels of protein. Irregular periods or inadequate blood flow can result but can be cleared up when those issues are addressed.

Migraines, can also be caused by certain food allergies and sensitivities which cause inflammation which in turn shows as migraine. Trigger food can be dairy, pork, beef, salt, certain oils like canola, corn or palm oil, and certain food additives. Magnesium is essential to relax blood vessels, which can protect you from painful migraines. Many people are deficient in Magnesium. It is found in almonds, cashews, brown rice, black beans and peas. Other help will come from CoQ10 and Lemon Balm. Herbal chamomile tea is good for headaches in general. If the headache feels cold, take Chamomile and Rosemary tea together.

Care is required in cases of persistent migraine or unexplained headache. It could be a problem in the kidneys and could well manifest in high blood pressure. If condition persists seek professional advice.

Mucous, is a crucially important body fluid, but in excess it is particularly annoying and even distressing to many people. Mucous is part of the immune response, so when the body detects a compound such as an allergen or food that is unsuitable for body chemistry the immune system kicks in to bathe the cells in mucous and through that protect the cells from danger.

Same applies when undigested food builds up in the stomach, the body reacts by producing mucous as protection. The problem arises when too much of one trigger or too many triggers at once build-up, the protective mucous becomes a problem in itself. A homeopathic preparation, Mucous Liquescence is very good for expelling excess Mucous.

Multiple Sclerosis, a condition with symptoms with slurred speech, diminished vision, fatigue, loss of balance, and inability to walk properly. Sufferers had many coinfections including viral, fungal and bacterial infections and mercury poisoning. Detoxification of all the compounds is essential. Use plant source Omega 3 and Amino acids to support the CNS. Curcumin relieves pain and inflammation.

Nail Polish/Varnish, are toxic compounds and so their use should be minimised. Apart from the user of polish, I found Beauty Therapists often suffered from digestive issues and constipation which resulted from remover fluid used in cleaning the paint from the nails.

Osteoporosis, the name given to bone thinning and becoming porous like. It results from a loss of nutrients particularly Calcium and Vitamin D. Diet is a big factor as high phosphorous levels in food restrict calcium uptake, so minimise foods with high levels of phosphorous. Homeopathy is also helpful. Suitable exercise is important to keep bones strong.

Parkinson's, a condition in the brain cells which may result from inability to produce dopamine. Symptoms include slight tremor or shaking of the head and difficulty walking or speaking. Add fruit to your diet especially coloured berries, and apples. Also include artichoke for better cognitive health. Homeopathy can be a great help to cognitive health.

Pregnancy, is a crucial time in a couples life. In the toxic times in which we live couples should plan pregnancy from a health point of view. I recall in the 1970s young women talked about birth at different times of year for tax advantages or avoidance of a summer pregnancy. However for the time we live now both partners should have a six month detox plan to clear chemicals and metals from the body. It is best get professional guidance to start on that aspect.

A healthy diet is important before and during pregnancy. Include adequate healthy fats, oily fish twice a week and perhaps add Omega 3 fish oil which will help mother and baby, Vitamin D is very important. If parasites occur during pregnancy I suggest homeopathy because of its safety. Avoid wormwood and other of medicinal herbs unless you have testing in advance.

Peripheral Neuropathy, a troublesome condition usually showing up as a tingling sensation, sensitivity, numbness or pain in the feet or hands or both. Loss of muscle function would be the most serious outcome. There are many different varieties of neuropathies such as motor and sensory caused by damage to the nerve endings and malfunction in the Central Nervous System (CNS). Causes are many such as toxicity from medications, diabetes or even injury to a single nerve ending. As always finding the cause or source of the problem will be the first step in resolving the issues. So diet or injury may need to be addressed. Diabetic neuropathy would probably be the most serious form of neuropathy so that can be addressed through a combination of diet and medication. To sooth the feet take a foot bath every night with Epsom salts added. Homeopathic remedies worked very well for many of my clients in providing relief.

Planet health, is crucially important to human and animal health. The damage to the ozone layer, the disappearance of traditional forests, the disappearance of lakes, the pollution of rivers and oceans and the disturbance of ecosystems all combine and impact badly on the health of all species. We need to increase awareness, raise public consciousness of those issues. We need to in-

form every person we can to be aware of the damage that has been done and continues to be done to the planet. Of course we can influence this in a number of ways. We can call on our politicians to take action through legislation. That's a slow process. At family and individual level we can do more, we can start tomorrow. We can do so through our purchasing power. We can ask in the shop for organic produce. We can move our purchasing elsewhere, with limitation for sure, if they don't respond in a sensible way. We can ask retailers to reduce plastic packaging or just refuse to buy a plastic wrapped product. We can cut down the use of fossil fuels. We can convert our heating systems and motor vehicles to more eco - friendly fuels. Our future is in our hands.

Relaxation, valerian tincture can promote sleep, calm relax muscles. Also, Ginseng, Echinacea, and Vitamin B Complex can be helpful. Magnesium helps with hyperactivity. Suitable exercise is important and maybe Yoga or Meditation.

Restless Legs, indicate a deficiency in Iron, Vitamin B12 and Folic Acid. Massage the legs with a mixture of lavender and sandalwood essential oils, blended in a Ground Nut Oil before going to bed at night. (Caution - avoid groundnut oils if suffering from nut allergies.) The condition may indicate a deficiency in minerals such as Zinc, Calcium or Magnesium.

Sleep. Adequate sleep is essential for quality of life, for vitality, for cognitive health and brain function. People need 7 to 9 hours each night to rejuvenate and recover adequately. I would not recommend more than 9 hours. Inability to sleep or waking up at 2.00AM indicates adrenal fatigue or stress so you will need to resolve the adrenal issue. If you wake up mid sleep, anxious and restless;

- Try Arsenicum album.
- Aconite or Rock Rose are good if you experience nightmares.

- Nux vomica can help combat the effects of too much caffeine or stress.
- Valerian, Passion flower, Lemon balm and Hops all have sedative properties also so check which works best for you.

People read or watch TV for some hours. I recommend against both. Avoid stimulants such as coffee and alcohol as they will keep you awake. To create a good flow of energy in your bedroom, cover any mirrors that show your reflection while you are in bed. Avoid lights at night as we need darkness for a minimum period, ideally 8 hours. Use warm colours to decorate your bedroom. Avoid troublesome films or stimulating TV programmes before bed time. Best even to avoid telephone calls from friends as the conversation can play over in your mind and cause loss of sleep. If you are buying a new bed, choose a wooden frame as it is less likely to be affected by electromagnetic stress than a metal frame.

Shingles, a painful a debilitating condition which mostly effects people in the senior years of life. The outward symptoms are skin rashes which can occur on several parts of the body accompanied by pain, fever, headache, rash, itch, in-flammation and fatigue. The itch can move from one part of the body to another. However shingles can be present without rashes where it attacks the nervous system.

Shingles is due to a virus from the herpes zoster species which can be dormant for years and strikes when the immune system is depressed for any reason including stress. The best approach is therefore to take preventative measures particularly a supported immune system. Take Vitamin C supplements regularly. At the on-set of winter take Thymus as the thymus gland is crucial to healthy immunity. When the infection occurs I found that homeopathy offers the best prospect of clearance of the virus. Lobelia is also helpful for the virus. In addition take Zinc, Magnesium and Selenium as they may each be needed to support immunity.

A home remedy (*taken from my mothers notes*) that has worked effectively for many people is as follows;

Sulphur - 6 teaspoons
Bextarter - 6 teaspoons
Mustard powder - 3 teaspoons
Brown sugar - 6 teaspoons
Olive oil - 6 table spoons

Blend all powders together and grind to a fine paste. Add the Olive oil and stir gently until consistent. Store in a glass jar. Apply once daily to effected areas of the body.

Sore Throats, Gargle with Vit. C Liquescence at first sign. Drink hot water with slice of lemon. Wear a blue scarf around neck.

Stomach Ulcers, are small but painful sores on the lining of the stomach or intestines. There are a range of symptoms such as vomiting, nausea, weight loss, gas and bloating. Check for bacterial infection as Helicobactor Plyori can be a cause. Diet will be a factor so minimise or delete for a period animal protein and replace with plant protein. Some clients found chewing on green banana leaves helpful.

Stress, one of the big health issues of our time contributing to many other chronic conditions including mental and emotional disorders, cancer and heart disease. Develop daily practices to contain and control stress levels, such as a regular walk, suitable exercise, games, integration with people, meditation and prayer. If your occupation or relationships are contributors to your stress it is important to examine both.

Surgery, can be planned or may come up suddenly. Best be prepared with optimum immunity. Surgery is the same as injury in energy medicine terms. The wound is an injury which interferes with normal energy flow. For a few days after surgery, say 4 to 6 you should take an injury remedy which will get energy flow moving again and will enhance wound healing. Homeopathy would be the best alternative for antibiotics to control infection. Use nutrients for recovery and recuperation.

Swelling on the Knees. Swelling on the knees is frequent and other joints may also be affected. This is a combination of fluid accumulation and inflammation which makes walking painful and distressing. Grate raw cabbage finely, wrap in cheese-cloth and secure the ends so that the cabbage cannot escape. Alternatively make a sack out of cheese-cloth, large enough to cover the afflicted area. Then cover with cling film and wrap a towel around it. Every night make a new compress. Do not expect results until after the third day.

Swollen Limb, if you have a swollen limb, place a cotton bag or cotton sock filled with washing soda on the affected area and leave it till it has all melted which could take up to 8 hours. Make sure you place a towel next to the skin first, before you put the bag with washing soda on.

Threadworm Remedy, one lemon, ½ pint of water, 2 tablespoons honey. Crush the peel, pulp and pips of the lemon. Cover with water and steep for 2 hours. Strain through a sieve, pressing the lemon to extract all the liquid. Discard the pulp. Add honey and drink before going to bed.

Thyroid Function, is important to good health. However if the thyroid gland is not able to produce the necessary hormones, dysfunction results. It falls into two categories as follows:

• **Underactive**: It is influenced by temperature, excitement, fear, anger, physical exertion, skin and hormone function. Symptoms of underactivity are cold hands and feet, slow pulse, depression, lack of energy, dry thick skin, abnormal hair loss, constipation, slow thinking, mental dullness, unable to lose weight, poor resistance to infection, thick brittle nails.

• **Overactive**: is reflected in low weight, rapid pulse, hypertension, staring eyes, swollen ankles and/or feet. B1 vitamins can sometimes help to restore Thyroid function.

Iodine deficiency is associated with thyroid dysfunction making it unable to produce hormones. This can be caused by viral infection especially EBV. This will need detox. Healthy thyroid is also dependent on healthy adrenal function. Address the iodine deficiency with iodine rich food in your diet, particularly sea vegetables or kelp. Yogurt, cheese, potatoes and strawberries are also good food sources. You can also take supplements, indeed supplements will be necessary in many cases and could include;

• Bladderwrack or kelp which is rich in iodine.
• Vitamin B1 can help to restore thyroid function.
• Chromium which helps the endocrine system and helps prevent weight gain.
• Zinc which treats infections and supports hormonal health.
• Magnesium and Selenium are essential to stimulate production of thyroid hormone.
• B Complex which is beneficial for the nervous system.
• Lemon balm which treats viral infection.
• Licorice root is also effective as it is antiviral and helpful for the adrenal glands.
• Homeopathy can be very helpful for infection control and micro nutrient absorption.

To improve thyroid function yourself, do the following exercise: Keep head straight, put whole hand around one side of throat, tap with hand and hum at same time. Do this for 5 mins, and then repeat on opposite side, do twice daily.

Tinnitis, which is known by a ringing sensation in the ear and may give a heavy feel to the ear and surrounding facial area. I found EBV infection in many cases. Homeopathy is helpful to clear the virus and restore balance.

Toothache. Chew a piece of ginger. You can also chew on a few cloves or put 2 drops of Clove essential oil on cotton wool and pack around the aching tooth.

Ulcerated acne, boils, eczema and psoriasis. You will need 2 quarts' apple cider vinegar, 8 grams of garlic, freshly mashed and 1 gram of horseradish, grated. Place herbs in the cider vinegar and leave to stand in a warm place for 12 hours. Remove to a cold place and let it stand for a further 12 hours. Strain and use 1 tablespoon, four times daily. Psoriasis is indicative of autoimmune disorder so you may need to attend to the Immune System and the Nervous System.

Protruding veins on the hands. Protruding veins on your hands do not look too pretty. In order to ease them, and in many cases erase them, this is what you do. Feel the back of your head three fingers wide off the upper rim of your ears. Press the left side of your head only. It will hurt. Hold it for one minute, twice daily and the protruding veins on the hands will disappear from several weeks to several months.

Various issues,
- Foot turning out – lack of calcium.
- Problem swallowing – cranial nerves.
- Dry skin – can be liver congestion.
- Dryness in mouth – can be lack of calcium, zinc or magnesium.
- Lump in throat – deficiency of fatty acids.
- White coating on back of tongue, usually caused by gas in the bowel. Try Sodium phosphate.

Verruca, or planter wart is a viral infection which can be picked up in pools or gyms. Homeopathy is good to clear the virus. Other options to try are,
- Clean the verruca with fresh dandelion milk.
- Put lemon juice and crushed garlic on a piece of banana skin and apply to the affected area, repeat until verruca clears.
- Take Causticum 30c for 5 days. Walk on sea sand and it will help draw out the verruca.
- Other cures, rub with black banana skin, or grapefruit extract.
- If it is removed surgically it will grow again and will eventually leave a hole in the foot.

Vertigo, take Magnesium Phosphate or Potassium Phosphate when symptoms arise.

Viral Infections. A health immune system is your first line of defence. Adequate calcium stocks are essential, but be aware that magnesium is required to absorb and hold calcium. Zinc strengthens the immune system and selenium the nervous system. I found that homeopathy was the most effective treatment where viral infections were a problem as it was fastest to give relief. Lemon balm and Red clover were valuable antiviral and antibacterial herbs. Curcumin helped with inflammation and pain relief.

Warts, split potato in two and rub over wart. Use the other half of the potato for your dinner. Do this for 3 nights. Also helpful is to apply onion juice to warts twice daily.

Weak Wrists, wrap pure wool around wrists.

Weeping, ignatia is excellent when the weepy state is recurring. Weeping can be useful but can also indicate an underlying emotional state which needs attention. If the condition is persistent then you should seek advice.

Winter Flu, becomes a concern for many especially the elderly. I have had many clients ask me for advice on the Flu Vaccine and many offered their opinions and experiences.

Clients tell of the experiences of their parents, particularly the numbers who receive the Vaccine but still get the flu. I believe that vaccines deplete the natural immune system and receiving vaccinations regularly, even annually can only be harmful in the longer term. However it is an individual decision for each person and their doctor.

For younger and middle aged people it is best to maintain a healthy immune system through a healthy diet and the avoidance of toxic substances which reduce immunity. This can be stress, smoking, excess alcohol, inadequate sleep or exercise. Take supplementary Vit C and /or Thymus which will boost immunity and reduce your risk of flu infection. In Sept/Oct, take Vit D3 as it is power full as an immune protector.

Detoxification

Over the past half century, the environment and the planet in general have become degraded. This has resulted from industrialisation, increased use of chemicals, changes in farming and food production methods and an ever-increasing use of toxic compounds in buildings, household's materials, foods, cosmetics and medications. Many of those compounds have made their way into body and damaged various organs and compromised the immune system.

Detoxification on a regular basis is essential so as to maintain organ integrity and overall body health. Homeopathy, which is an energy-based medicine, is a key element in the detoxification process as it eliminates toxins at the cellular level. Herbs can also be very useful as they detoxify at tissue and organ level.

Daily Simple Detox

Before going to bed, take a bath with 2 cups vinegar and ¼ cup Epsom salts. Increase this gradually to 6 cups of vinegar and 1 cup Epsom salts. It is important to take shower in the morning to wash this off.

Liver Detox (blurred vision and stuffed liver)

The liver is the primary organ for the processing of compounds including toxins and clearing them from the system. It always needs support. There are several things that can be done to aid the liver, as follows:

- 1oz of peppermint, 1oz elderflowers, brew these in 1½ pint of boiling water and drink every half hour until liquid is used up.

- A wonderful tonic for your liver is right in your back yard. Take a small handful of dandelion leaves. Place in a blender with a carton of cranberry juice and after liquidising, take 6ozs twice daily and repeat for ten days.

- A combination tonic that's good for the liver is dandelion, horehound, sweet flag, flaxseed and burdock. Simmer in 2 pints of water and take 1oz after meals.

- Fresh lemon juice in a cup of hot water taken first thing in the morning will empty your gallbladder and freshen the liver.

Procedure to Detoxify the Liver, Bile and the Kidney System

Prepare by opening six cans of Coca-Cola 48 hours before you start.

Day 1 - Drink six cans of flat coke in two hours (20 mins per can) on an empty stomach.

Day 2 - Take one red grapefruit and one lemon (peel and remove stones) and two cloves of garlic, place in liquidiser and shred until soft pulp is achieved. Take pulp on empty stomach.

Day 3 - Drink 2ozs of olive oil mixed with the juice of 2 lemons, on an empty stomach.

Day 4 - Take 2 teaspoons of Epson salts dissolved in boiling water, on empty stomach.

Day 5 - Take a day off.

Days 6 to 11 - Take half a carton of organic apple pulp each day for these six days or three peeled apples (cooking or organic) on an empty stomach.

A System of Body Draining for Personal and Home use as follows:

1. Drain the head by tapping hard with the heels of both hands.
2. Massage the indentations on the head behind the top of ears.
3. Massage the centre of the forehead above the nose and drain off.
4. Drain above and below the eyes in an outward direction into the side of neck.
5. Work the points at the corner of the nose and mouth and drain into the side of neck.
6. Pinch the jaws firmly up to the hairline.
7. Drain from behind the top of the ears in a straight line down the side of the neck. Do this by drawing the fingers slowly but firmly along the skin to the clavicle.
8. Place hands around the neck so that the tips of the fingers are almost touching the spine at the rear neck and the heels of the palm are almost touching at the front of the neck. Squeeze the back of the neck very rapidly five times. Without moving the hands, squeeze the front of the neck five times very rapidly.
9. Drain the rear of the neck by tapping firmly. It is best to have someone do this for you.
10. Work the fingers into the arm pits.
11. Drain the front of the body by thumbing the breast bone from shoulder to shoulder.
12. Thump the heart area a few times.
13. Press all fingers in under the breastbone, and then bend the body up and down with the fingers in place.

14. Work the liver vigorously with the heel of the hand. It is located mainly on the right-hand side of the stomach.
15. Do the same with the Pancreas which is located on the left-hand side of the stomach.
16. Place the right hand under the right side at the base of the rib cage. Press firmly with the heel of the hand and bring firmly down to the naval. Repeat this five times and drain off.
17. With the heels of the hand on each side of the rib cage, with pressure move both hands downward to meet at the naval.
18. Drain the back of the neck with a roller (if available).
19. Drain shoulders (at rear) by thumping.
20. Drain the lungs from the rear by thumping (in the upper neck).
21. Drain the kidneys from the rear by thumping (in the lower back).
22. Work the fingers vigorously into both sides of the groin.
    Put both hands around the left ankle. With one thumb above the other apply pressure (only with the thumbs) drawing the thumbs up the inside of the leg to the groin.
23. Now with the thumb on the ankle of the same (left) foot, repeat the exercise as in 23.
24. Drain the right leg as you did the left. Put towel in groin and do 10 leg pull ups. Hold in groin and count to 10.
25. Take a deep breath and hold, force out the stomach, count to five.
26. When resting raise your feet on a chair to drain.
27. Repeat No 16.

Your face and body under your control

What benefits should you expect from a healthy body with all organs at optimum function? You could expect the following:

1. Improvement in alertness and mental function.
2. Stimulating of pituitary gland and hormone function.
3. Improvement in facial skin and muscles.
4. Toxin removal through better kidney function.
5. Improvement in digestive processes and colon function.
6. Assistance in renewal of blood cells.
7. Stimulating the lungs and oxygen supply.
8. Improvement in libido and sex drive.
9. Aiding the liver and lymphatic system.
10. Nervous system enhancement.
11. Reduce weight around hips, thighs and stomach.

Chapter Five

Essential Foods

Essential and Non Essential Foods

Food is the source of live, you are what you eat. But all foods are not the same. Try to consume organic foods, fruit and vegetables as much as possible. This will not always be easy, but if enough people ask, then consciousness is raised and suppliers will try harder to meet demand. Where animal source food is concerned, use free range grass fed lamb and beef. Ask for organic or free range chicken. Wild fish is much safer than farmed fish as the later has colouring added so as to give it a better appearance. Organic supply is the best guarantee that chemical fertilising and the use of antibiotics in feedstuffs is avoided.

Apple, a general all round health food, helpful for liver and gallbladder. Good for brain health and relief of constipation. Scrape out the flesh and use as a poultice when necessary.

Apple Cider Vinegar, Take one spoon of apple cider vinegar in a large glass of water first thing in the morning on empty stomach. This invigorates and helps to detoxify the body.

Apricots, good source of magnesium, helps as detox for liver and pancreas and control of infectious agents like mold, yeast and candida.

Asparagus, helpful for oesophagus, fatty tumours and urinary system.

Avocado, poor on taste but very helpful in cases of digestive disorders like IBS, female health, adrenal fatigue and oesophageal health.

Banana, high in potassium and other minerals like magnesium, copper and boron. Can be mucous forming for some people but nevertheless good for fungus control and can relieve anxiety and improve sleep.

Barley, abundance of B12, good for heart, the kidneys and the immune system. It is also helpful for the nervous system. Take one mug of barley and 8 mugs of water and boil for about one hour. Leave to cool in the pot and strain. Keep this in the fridge and drink one mug, twice daily, morning and night.

Barley Water, to make one mug of Pearl Barley, put pearl barley into 4 pints of cold water. Bring to boil and simmer for 1 hour. When cold strain and place in fridge. Drink one Mug every morning.

Beans (Green), helps detox metals and good for pancreas health.

Beet Fibre, good for colon health.

Beetroot, contains Vitamin E. Daily use, improves blood flow, clears body of bacteria and parasite waste, good for the lymph nodes and the heart. Excellent for blood health and prevention of chronic health conditions. Cucumber is a healthy complementary food.

Beetroot Booster, Boil beetroots with the skin on, when cooked remove skin. Beetroot is now ready to eat. Alternatively the skin can be removed from the raw beetroots, then grate the beetroot flesh. It can then be added to salads and dishes and eaten in its raw or fresh state. Note: Always use fresh beetroot and avoid the vacuum packed produce.

Berries, coloured berries are important and health giving.

- Blue berries should be given more prominence in our though processes followed by black berries and cherries. Blueberries are important for brain health.
- Cranberries are good for the kidneys and urinary tract problems.
- Cherries are high in zinc and iron and will boost the endocrine system. Cherries are good for constipation relief and will clean the bowels.

Pick wild berries or better still encourage market gardeners and farmers to include them in their crop list. They can be eaten raw or cooked to make delightful deserts.

Bladderwrack, or kelp is derived from seaweed and is rich in many minerals including iodine, calcium, magnesium, sodium and potassium. It is a very important for thyroid health so as to prevent underactive thyroid

Bread, an essential food but more important still is healthy bread. What are the choices:

• **Spelt flour** is on the way back, thankfully. Spelt is a member of the wheat species but has a larger protective hull which is expensive to process. It was widely used up to the early decades of the last century but went into decline because of processing costs which made wheat and rye more profitable for producers. I urge everybody to support the spelt producers. It contains more vitamins and amino acids than wheat flour. It contains a lower level of gluten than wheat but people with celiac condition should still be cautious.

• **Sourdough** is another good option. It is the preparation of the bread that makes the difference. You will need a mix to start with, add it to your floor and water and let stand for about 10 hours before baking. Whilst the bread is very tasty the key advantage is the avoidance of yeast which in itself is troublesome to many people.

• **White flour** has been the dominant flour for the last century or more. The introduction of the steam roller resulted in the removal of wheat germ with its essential vitamins, minerals, amino acids and fatty acids. This kept the flour from spoiling during storage. The bran present was also lost. Another problem was the addition of bleach, a toxin in itself, to whiten the flour. White flour bakery products will usually contain baking powder instead of the healthier baking soda. Baking powder is a chemical mix, it may contain aluminium and will surely have added white sugar. All of this means white flour is low in nutritional value and is troublesome to many by causing constipation and digestive problems. For a healthy diet, avoid white flour from the mill.

Broccoli, probably the most valuable vegetable available which is rich in Vitamin E. Helps removes toxins. Eat one or two stems a day. Combined with one capsule of Vitamin E, it will s will reduce the acid level in the stomach and alkalise the body.

Chicken is a good food, but look for organic or free range. The taste is better but it is worth the effort and the higher price to avoid the Cage raised chickens. The production methods used for poultry meat production for the past 50 years has been an insult to our humanity.

Cabbage, has many healthful benefits;

- It stimulates the immune system so it helps to fight infection, eaten regularly it prevents constipation and acts as a good internal cleanser.
- Cabbage contains Vitamin E and beta carotene so is good for stomach, the lungs, ulcers and hiatus hernia.
- Cabbage juice is good for bites, acne, burns and cold sores.
- Can be used in a poultice and applied to the lower abdomen, relieves fluid retention and soothes cystitis. The poultice can also draw out cysts and under skin growths. Use fresh leaves only.
- Can also be used as a poultice for ulcers. Pour hot water over cabbage leaf, let cool and apply to ulcer.
- Cabbage Water, 1 Mug per day, will reduce the acid levels in the stomach and alkalise the body.

Carrots, contains Vitamin A and E, rich in Niacin and B12, lowers cholesterol, cleans blood cell walls, opens capillaries and arteries and fights infections.

Cayenne Pepper, is an effective to detox and reduce acidity. It controls bacteria, enhances blood circulation and helps in regulation of blood sugar.

Celery, an excellent all round and versatile food rich in mineral salts. Eat a stem as a healthy snack between meals. Chop and include in a salad. Boil slightly as your ordinary veg for dinner. As a detox drink, boil 4 stems in four litres of water,

let go cold, store in fridge and drink a litre a day. If you do this continually for 14 days, leave it then for 30 days. Another method is to juice fresh celery first thing in the morning. On an empty stomach drink while fresh and it will enhance production of hydrochloric acid, which is essential for gut and digestive health. Celery is good for gout and joint pain.

Coconut, an excellent food that can also be used topically. Coconut is a saturated fat which lowers cholesterol and is protective for heart health and brain health. It is very suitable for cooking as it remains stable at high temperature giving it an important advantage over other oils.

Cucumber, is a hydrating vegetable and therefore good for the liver, good for kidney cleansing and infection control especially during viral infections like shingles. Use for reproductive health and infertility. Frest cucumber juice can be very healthful.

Fats and Oils. Good fats, are essential in the diet as they as they provide energy and essential nutrients for general health and in particular for brain, heart and joint function. Fats are classified as saturated fats or unsaturated. Saturated fats which you will recognise by the fact that they are solid at room temperature, are found in red meats such as lamb and beef, dairy products, particularly butter. However I recommend that red meats should be consumed at moderate levels, say small portions once per week.

Unsaturated fats are also recommended and have been the darlings of nutritional enthusiasts in recent decades. Sources of those fats are oily fish like salmon, herring, mackerel and sardines. Vegetable sources are olives, avocados, walnuts, hazelnuts and flax seeds. Drizzle a spoon of olive oil over your green salad. It will make the salad more tasty but more important-ly it will enhance absorption of the essential nutrients in your greens.

Flaxseed, is good for the bowel and may lower cholesterol. It is important to grind the flaxseeds. Alternatively take flaxseed oil. Flaxseed tea is very soothing to an irritated digestive tract. It coats, heals and nourishes. Take 2 tablespoons of flaxseed to one quart of water. Simmer for twenty minutes, strain and drink 1 cup of the warm mixture every two hours. For best results, alternate with carrot juice. One hour carrot juice, the next hour flaxseed tea.

Food Production, in my opinion has been at the heart of poor health conditions and chronic illness for many people for most of the past 50 years. Intensive use of land, two crops per year, excess fertilisation, the use of herbicides and pesticides have all combined to damage the soil with knock on damage to output, plants and animals alike. The increasing levels of industrial food processing and the addition of chemical compounds for taste, colour and shelf life extension have also been damaging. The use of antibiotics in animal and poultry production, whether to prevent infection or speed up weight or maturity is particularly objectionable.

I encourage everybody interested in health to voice their concerns about such practices and have them brought under control. If producers want better quality food they could fertilise the soil with natural compounds like sea vegetables. To the diet of animals they could add natural compounds like Beta Glucans from mushrooms or oats or Omega 3 from sea vegetables all of which will give better quality meat.

Fruits, send confusing signals to some people because they are sweet and therefore contain sugar. Fruit sugar is not the same as processed sugar that is added to beverages. Whilst the fruit contains sugar it is the whole fruit that contains the healing properties. Fruits should be a key element in the diets of people with serious conditions such as cancer and brain disorders. Combine a selection of 2 or 3 fruits such as banana, coloured berries, mango, apple, pear, kiwi, or melon into a smoothie. To dampen the sweet taste add a helping of greens like kale, spinach or celery. An apple and celery smoothie daily would be a great help.

Garlic, good for blood, (anti-clotting) heart, digestive problems, the immune system and helps to kill parasites. It is a substance which kills bacteria which is known to cause many digestive problems. Crush 2 to 3 cloves of garlic and put into socks day or night. It will be absorbed into the blood and will help he immune system and help kill parasites. Suck a small clove of peeled garlic for one hour and do not bite it, then discard it. This is good for sore throats and problems with the oesophagus. Garlic is best used raw, crushed or chewed. The bitter taste is not felt if you insert the clove into an olive.

Ginger, can be used as a mix with certain dishes, as a hot water drink or in capsule form. It has been used in healing for centuries. It is helpful for inflammation and pain. It enhances memory. It is a good blood tonic and can prevent harmful clotting. It can be used in the fight against diabetes and cancers such as breast and ovarian.

Grapes, promote good health, are good for liver health and the digestive system, for blood health and tumour prevention. Red grapes are high in phosphorous whereas white grapes are low in phosphorous.

Green Tea, detoxes the body, lowers cholesterol, helps with weight loss and may help prevent cancer of the breast, prostate, stomach, mouth and oesophagus.

Kale, contains Vitamin E, is a good cleansing food, is good for healing wounds and contains 40 times more calcium than milk.

Kiwi, an excellent fruit and is to the fruit family, what broccoli is to the vegetable family. This fruit is high in amino acids, trace minerals and Vitamin C. Use for prevention and treatment of diabetes as it helps regulate blood sugar levels. Use for digestive disorders such as bloating, belching, acid reflux, flatulence, gout, mood disorders, adrenal fatigue and hormonal problems.

Lemon, tonic, diuretic, antiseptic, and detoxifier. A slice of lemon first thing in the morning in hot water will help:

- Clear the digestive system and stimulate the liver and empty the gallbladder.
- Digestive problems such as nausea, constipation, heartburn, hiccups, worms, sore throats, asthma, water retention, arthritis, rheumatism, bleeding.
- Helps with sunburn, cleanse greasy skin and sooths chapped lips.
- A tablespoon of lemon juice in water half an hour before eating, sipped slowly will aid digestion.
- A tablespoon of lemon juice in a cup of hot water will make a gargle for sore throat, repeat every hour in acute cases.

Magnetized Water, is an excellent health maintenance measure. It can also be helpful during treatments for illness. Up to four glasses of water can be taken ideally before meals. North Pole magnetized water is good for external complaints like wounds, swollen eyes, spots, cuts and eye infections. In the case of swollen eyes or eye infection bathe with magnetized water. It helps the digestive system, regulates bowel movement, helps with internal infections and helps clear the kidneys. It has a very calming effect on the nervous system.

Milk, is so firmly embedded in the psyche of the nation it would be impossible to ignore. Nature established that milk was the immediate lifesaver of the new born, provided on the spot by its mother. It was intended to be a transition food until such time as the young could live on conventional rations. With commercial farming, food processing and advertising it has become a commodity for profits and control. People are told "milk is good for." However my experience provides me with mixed feelings summarised as follows:

- Mothers milk is best and absolutely essential for babies as it sets the foundation for a healthy digestive system.
- Cow's milk is a growing problem for many because of lactose intolerance. Lactose is a form of sugar found in milk.
- Casein is another substance, a protein in milk which is difficult to digest.
- Children are sensitive to milk and dairy products which shows in the form of allergies, skin problems and mucous accumulation. When cow's milk is removed from the diet those problems often disappear.

- Goat's milk or sheep milk could provide better alternatives.
- Milk is recommended for bone health because it's a good source of calcium.

However milk it is also a source of phosphate and as calcium uptake is controlled by phosphate levels in the blood, I cannot see the benefit of milk for bone health.

Mustard and Black Mustard Seeds, a much misunderstood and little known vegetable with enormous health giving potential. Some of its benefits include:

- Mustard has antibacterial and antifungal properties. 1 teaspoon of black mustard seed every morning taken with a little water will reduce fat levels in the blood stream which reduces the risk of clogging of arteries.
- Mustard stimulates circulation, fights colds, flu, chilblains and depression.
- A mustard seed infusion can relieve chest infections, rheumatism and arthritis.
- A teaspoon of mustard in a cup of hot water will provoke vomiting and therefore relieve poisoning.
- Use an infusion of mustard as an antiseptic gargle for sore throats and tonsillitis.
- Mustard seed infused in hot water will relieve hiccups.
- Hot mustard plaster applied like a compress will relieve congestion and reduce inflammation in arthritis and rheumatism by drawing blood to the surface of the skin.
- A hot foot bath containing 1 tablespoon of dried mustard powder can relieve congestion in the head and lungs by drawing the blood downward.

Mustard seed infusion, steep one teaspoon of ground black mustard seeds in a cup of boiling water and drink three times a day.

Mustard plaster, crush a handful of black mustard seeds and mix with a little flour. If black mustard seeds are not available, use powdered mustard. Add enough warm water to make into a paste. Put into a cotton cloth and place over the affected area. If the skin is sensitive, rub a little olive oil before you apply the plaster. Do not use mustard oil as it could be toxic.

Mustard foot bath: after a long walk in which the feet feel flat and hot or when cold seems to eat into the bones around the ankles, a foot bath relieves and revitalises the whole body. Two (2) teaspoons of ground mustard powder with 2 tablespoons olive oil. Mix the mustard and oil together and put in water, soak the feet for 20 minutes. Relax, close your eyes and allow the warmth to spread up your legs, through your body. Dry well and keep the feet warm afterwards.

Oats, the familiar breakfast grain is a wholegrain natural fibre. Oat Bran lowers cholesterol and is very useful for healthy skin and the avoidance of eczema. For skin care you can use an oat bath as follows:

Method I: Boil about 1 pint of water and add 3 handfuls of oatmeal. Let it simmer for about 20 minutes, strain and add the liquid to a bathtub of water. Sit in the water for approximately 30 minutes.

Method II: Put about 3 handfuls of oatmeal in a large knee stocking, tie it and hang it under the tap of your bath and let the hot water run on it. Cool the bath to the appropriate temperature before you get in. The sock with the oatmeal can be used again. For children apply oatmeal wrapped in a clean cloth directly to the body. Caution is required as oats may be mucous forming for some metabolisms so have a Kinesiology test if in doubt.

Onion, one of the medicinal foods of history with multiple applications:

- Onion juice can be used as ear drops, 2 drops in ear to reduce infection or poured on cotton wool.
- Onion juice mixed with honey for chest infection, sinuses, bronchitis, sore throats, colds and flu.
- A slice of raw onion helps to take the pain out of wasp and bee stings. Apply every half hour.
- Use onion on chilblains as a poultice.
- Apply onion juice on warts twice daily.

- To combat gout, apply poultice of grated onion and cover with bandage. Change every 3 hours. The onion juice facilitates drawing out acid from the body.
- Leave cut onions in a sick room when there is somebody with a fever or cold. The onion will absorb the air-borne bacteria.
- In tincture format onion can be combined with garlic, lemon juice and brown sugar as a natural antibiotic.

Organic Foods, are crucial to healthy living. I recommend to every reader to talk to every farmer you know and encourage them to convert some or all of their output to organic produce. In addition I recommend you talk to your politicians and ask them to lobby the Government to provide subsidies as tax reliefs or grants to farmers to make that conversion. We have an abundance of  food, an over supply, in the developed world which is harmful to the environment and the planet. Because of its quality and contaminant level it is damaging to the health of many people.

I recommend that wherever possible, shop at your local Farmers Market. Encourage you Supermarket to stock organic produce and encourage every person to do likewise. When enough people ask they start to listen.

Parsley, another of the garden herbs which is not well understood for its many health benefits which include;

- High in Vit B12 which has mental health benefits.
- Has high iron content.
- Good for heart health and the immune system, so use it daily.
- Helps with detox of kidneys and bowel and prevents piles.
- Lowers blood pressure. In cases of severe BP use 2ozs per day.
- Rejuvenates the nerves.
- Use organic product where possible.

Parsnip, good for and helpful in cases of dairy intolerance.

Pork/Pig meat, a traditional Irish food for generations. However it is not a meat I recommend for regular use. If you have joint pains or stiffness then avoid pig meat products.

Potato, juice helps gallstones, colic, ulcers and indigestion. Raw potato soothes cuts, ulcers, skin rashes, sunburn, chilblains, and inflamed skin. Slice the potato and rub gently on area affected. For burns and sunburn apply one grated potato to 1 teaspoon of virgin olive oil and apply to the affected area. For internal use, peel four potatoes and boil the skins in a pint of water. Cool and drink daily for skin complaints.

Red meats, are an important part of our history, especially beef and lamb. I recommend a small portion once or twice a week. Animal fats including butter should be small part of overall fat content. Buy from a butcher.

Prunes, source of iron and good for constipation, especially prune juice.

Rose Hips, a very traditional remedy and a natural source of Vitamin C. It is an ideal anti-inflamamatory and immune booster which will help ward off and see us through infections and other troublesome conditions. Good also for emotional stressors like non friendy work colleagues, neighbours or family members. Use in cases of eye and ear infections, gum or dental problems, urinary tract and bladder infections.

To make your own syrup you will need 2 cups of Rose hips, 1 tablespoon of sugar, 4 ½ pints of water. Extract the juice from the Rose Hips. Have 3 pints of boiling water ready. Mix the Rose hips in a coarse mincer and place in boiling water. Bring to the boil again, then stand 15 minutes. Pour with a jelly bag. Return the syrup to saucepan and add the sugar. Boil for 1 minute and leave to stand for 10 minutes.

Spinach, Contains Vitamin E and Beta Carotene, which is a good cleanser. Also contains potassium, good for the heart and the liver. Spinach has 10 times more calcium than milk, so it can be described as 'king of the greens'.

Sprouts, good for mineral supply especially magnesium and selenium which promote immunity.

Sugar, in refined form is a food to be avoided. Technology enabled the extraction of white crystals from sugar beet and sugar cane thereby eliminating and nutrients that may have been present. As a sweetener it replaced other materials such as honey, maple syrup, barley malt or molasses. There are few processed foods on the market that do not contain added sugar ranging from bakery products, to processed meats, sauces, ketchup, chilled foods, fast foods, wines and beverages.

Sugar has a dreadful effect on physical, emotional and mental health. It interferes with calcium metabolism, stresses the pancreas, causes fat deposits to build up, produces unwanted stomach acids, depletes the body's store of calcium, magnesium, chromium and B Vitamins, depresses the immune system and effects brain function triggering mood swings, hyperactivity and aggressive behaviour in susceptible people.

The widespread use of sugar in the food chain is a failing by our elected leaders and the specialists that advise them in that they have permitting unlimited use of processed sugar together with targeted advertising of high sugar products to young children and adults alike.

Thistle tea, is very good for people who struggle with fever.

Tomato Juice, use ripe tomatoes. To each quart of pulp add, ½ pint of water, 1oz sugar, salt and pepper. Blend as you would a juice.

Turmeric, another of the versatile foods that can be used as a basic ingredient or as a food supplement. Curcumin is the key ingredient in turmeric, the yellow powder that makes your curry yellow. This spice can be used for flavourings, as a tea, a smoothie or beverage. In medicinal terms turmeric can be used as a digestive aid, an anti-inflammatory and for joint pain, arthritis, cancer and skin conditions.

Vegetables, like fruits are key to a healthy diet. Use green leafy for the most part, with preference for the above ground over the tuber. The later will tend to have more sugar and starch. Make your vegetable portion at least a third of your dinner plate. In cases of illness, increase the vegetable content at the expense of the meat or fish content. Use raw vegetables or near to raw where possible.

Examples would be onion and broccoli. Use vegetables imaginatively, such as mashed cauliflower instead of potatoes to reduce starch intake. For smoothies use raw greens combined with fruit such kiwi or mango.

Vinegar, contains acetic acid but is alkalising in nature. Vinegar is a very versatile commodity, as a health food, cleanser, detoxifier, has external use benefits and household cleanser. It is a source of potassium and magnesium. It is useful for controlling bacterial infection and for candida, can help with blood sugar and diabetes symptoms and can enhance digestion. Externally it can be used to give a shine in your hair. For household use freshen your fridge and provide a new look for your delph and cutlery among other uses.

You can make your own home vinegar if you can buy an acetic acid bacteria to which you add alcohol of your choice. This can be wine, beer or even fermented fruit juice. The acetic acid bacteria is a mother starter, a slime like substance from vinegar making, in the same way as butter milk is from churning cream, or whey from cheese making. To this substance add alcohol, cap, and let stand to mature. Apple cider is the best known and most popular vinegar.

Water, clean water alongside good food are the two most important elements of good health and therefore are the primary commodities in any home cure. Unfortunately, because of the prevalence of contamination you will need a home water filter under the kitchen sink. A good quality filter will eliminate 90% of the chemical and metal contaminants

from the water. That's a good start. Drink 1 to 2 litters per day. Avoid bottled water as it stands on shelves for far too long in plastic bottles.

Yogurt, is a low calorie protein food. Use natural yogurt that does not have sugar or other additives. My own favourite is Greek Style natural yogurt.

Food Groups – Important Combinations

Acidic Fruits: Oranges, Lemons, Pineapple, Grapefruit, Lime, Sour Grapes, Peaches, Sour Plums

Sub Acid Fruits: Pears, Sweet Peaches, Sweet Apples, Sweet Cherries, Sweet Plums

Sweet Fruits: Banana, Watermelon, Honeydew Melon, Nutmeg Melon, Honey Balls

Protein: Cereals, Beans, Peas, Soya, Avocado, Nuts

Carbs: All Cereals, Potatoes, Pumpkin, Chestnuts

Mild Starches: Cauliflower, Carrots, Beets, Broccoli

Sugars: White and Brown Sugar, Honey, Maple Syrup, Cane Syrup

Chapter Six

Favourite Herbs, Homeopathy, Oils and Nutrients

Herbs

Herbs have been used throughout history as foods, as preventative medicines and as medicinal products in themselves. When I started practice I could easily source many of the more specialised herbs which I could not grow myself. Now Government regulation has come into place and  many of the useful and essential herbs are on prescription or controlled in some other way. I feel this is an absurd approach to public health management which denies individuals and families the opportunity of enhancing or protecting their own health.

Hereunder are the herbs I have used and recommended although some are now on prescription or restricted in some other manner.

Antioxidants herbs, such as thyme, sage and rosemary which can be used in foods are particularly effective as anti-ageing remedies.

Black Cohosh, the best to help with female health issues. It is an excellent alternative to hormone replacement therapy (HRT).

Black Walnut, important for parasite control and people also use it for their post-Christmas detox and weight control efforts.

Birch leaves, good as kidney cleanser, especially if there are deposits in the kidney. Pick the leaves during May and dry carefully. To dry place in a pillow case and lie in front of the window with the sun shining in. Turn every day. Store in dry glass jar. Place one teaspoon in two cups of water, bring to the boil, simmer for 4 to 5 minutes. Allow to cool before drinking. You can reuse the leaves a few times.

Burdock, a bitter herb but very versatile and contains many essential trace minerals. It can be used as a blood cleanser, for liver health, as a kidney cleanser, helps urine flow, relieves arthritic pain and helps during the common cold. Use also for fibromyalgia, adrenal fatigue, pain relief, infections and cancers of the lung and thyroid.

Chamomile, has calming properties and contains calcium in a form that the cells can utilise.

Calcium Herbs, such as chamomile, horsetail, plantain, watercress and willow leaves are good sources of calcium.

Clove, a versatile herb that can be used as a tincture or oil and is anti- viral and anti- fungal, Clove is anti-inflammatory and is also soothing when used externally. An ordinary clove in hot water can be used to soothe sore throat

Comfrey, leaves are helpful for sore bones. Put the smooth side of the leaf to the skin for about 4 days and it will take the soreness away. Do not apply to broken skin. Another method is to boil the leaves and rub the liquid onto the affected part of the body. Comfrey is also very good as a natural fertilizer for flowers and vegetables and is easy to grow in a corner of your garden.

Coriander, an excellent herb for brain health. It is high in minerals like sodium, potassium and chloride which bind to metal toxins and carry them from the body for excretion. Use for anxiety, depression, dementia, Alzheimers, ADHD, autism, chronic fatigue and viral infections.

You can use it as a soup or chop up and spread over your soup or salad. A delightful presentation is as a pesto. Combine a mug of coriander with a mug of basil a glove of chopped garlic and blend in mixer. Add 2 spoons of Extra Virgin Olive Oil and a squeeze of lemon. Use as a dip or salad mix or on toasted sourdough.

Dandelion, another of the versatile herbs where leaf, stem and root can be used either in combination or separately. Whilst it is bitter it can be eaten cooked or raw, as a soup or salad or indeed dandelion wine or as a beverage. For therapeutic use it is good for spleen, liver and brain health, and particularly prostate health. It is a detoxifier and diuretic and provider of Vitamin A, as well as magnesium, selenium and silica. Dandelion and Burdock combined in tincture format are good for skin and bone health.

Echinacea, best known for its ability to help prevent and reduce the symptoms of cold and flu, but is also useful for clear skin, mouth ulcers, ear infections, gum disease, bronchitis and sore throats. It also boosts the immune system.

Essiac, detoxes the liver, purifies the blood and oxygenates the cells. A great remedy for boosting the immune system.

Gingko Biloba, increases blood circulation throughout the brain and whole body. Research suggests that it can improve memory and concentration. It can also help prevent circulatory problems and brain degeneration. We should all take it, especially if there is a history of Alzheimer's or senile dementia in the family. Take 100mls of Gingko Biloba for six weeks before you are due to fly, as it helps keep blood vessels dilated. Unfortunately it is a prescription herb.

Goldenseal, recommended for people who want to feel and look young and it also takes away sores and blemishes on the skin.

Hawthorne berry, is good herb for reproductive health especially the ovaries.

Horsetail, a versatile herb with many uses. It can be taken internally to stop bleeding from ulcers or heavy periods. It can be used as a poultice for boils and skin troubles. It can be used orally for brittle nails, bronchitis, cough, and infections.

Lavender is a delightful herb whether it is just to view in the garden or inhale the aroma of dried flower in the bathroom. For medicinal purposes dilute lavender oil with almond oil and massage into the knee for pain relief from osteoarthritis. Use a 50/50 mix and massage for up to 20 minutes.

Lemon Balm, a very effective herb with broad based therapeutic value. It is a valuable tonic for the nervous system. It assists brain function especially in cases of autism. It is beneficial for thyroid health and is anti-viral, especially in cases of EBV infection. Use if you feel tired or have problems concentrating or have a stressful event coming up.

Mistletoe, mistletoe is an excellent herb to soften muscles, treat bumps and fatty tumours and is a blessing for an overworked heart. Mistletoe is widely used as a cancer treatment in Germany and other countries, however it is a prescription medicine in Ireland.

Nettle leaf, another wild home grown useful herb for brain, blood, the nervous system and hormonal health. Make a soup, use as a salad, tincture, nettle tea or nettle wine if that takes your fancy. Add mint to make a tea. It is a most versatile herb, never refer to is as a weed to be destroyed. It is useful for a range of women's issues such as improving fertility, hormonal balancing, vaginal irritations, PMS, menstrual cramps, low adrenal function, viral infections, shingles, cervical and uterine cancers

Peppermint, an alkalizing herb and a good digestive aid.

Phosphorous Herbs, are good nerve co-ordinators and brain foods. Included are Sunflower seeds, Aniseed, Fenugreek, Watercress and Chickweed.

Potassium Herbs, are always very healing, which include Chamomile, Comfrey, Fennel, Nettle and Walnut.

Red Clover, another versatile herb high in nutrients like magnesium, manganese, selenium, iron and Vitamins A and B. Very good for the lymphatic system and for lymph drainage. Use for high blood pressure, hormonal problems like PMS and menopausal symptoms, constipation and/or loose stools and food allergies.

Rosemary, can be combined with many food dishes and extremely effective remedy to increase blood flow to the brain.

Rhodiola is an energising herb helpful for sports people and athletes, boosts energy helps adrenal function and provides relief from stress.

Sage, another food, very good to improve memory and good for female hormones.

Thuja, because of toxicity level it is recommended in homeopathic format only for oral or internal use. It can be used topically for warts.

Wormwood, another important herb for parasite control. However I recommend caution in its use. It is best if you use kinesiology for testing.

Herbal bags

Rosemary, Lavender and Tansy as a herbal mix can enhance a room or bathroom with a pleasant aroma. Tie in a decorative cloth bag for maximum effect.

Homeopathy

Adrenal Liquescence, important for menopausal women, fatigue, sleeping difficulties, stress and relief from allergies. Ideal for the active and intensive sports people. It is used as Rescue Remedy by many people.

Amalex, important remedy for detoxification of mercury and cellular cleansing.

BAC, useful for all kinds of bacterial infections. Mothers medicine chest remedy especially where there are children in the house.

B Complex Liquescence, provides enhanced mental energy and provides relief from moderate depression.

Calcium Liquescence, very important remedy for calcium and magnesium uptake and absorption as well as for bone and skeletal health.

China, (Cinchona officials), good for Uric Acid which causes gout and also indigestion.

Female Liquescence, good for female hormonal balance during both menses and menopause phases of life. Use also in cases of ovarian cysts.

Liver Liquescence, for liver support as it processes toxins for elimination.

Lycopodium, important for back pain, bowel problems and sciatica

Magnesium Liquescence, essential remedy as balancer and for calcium absorption. Also for headache due to elevated blood pressure, onset depression, muscle flexibility and bone health.

Rescue Remedy, Gives comfort and reassurance that you can cope, especially when you feel as though you cannot cope any longer. Is a special combination of Five Bach Flower remedies – Star of Bethlehem, Cherry, Plum, Clematis, and Rock rose. These remedies are to tackle emotions and offer a sense of calm. There is also Rescue Remedy Cream to help cuts and bruises; this is especially good for children.

Rhus Tox, short for Rhus toxicodendron, is a traditional remedy used for colds, flu symptoms like fever, muscle pains and aches. It is also used for skin conditions like rashes, shingles and blisters. In fact its all-round remedy for toxicity and detoxification.

Serdop, very important for stimulating serotonin dopamine levels and helping with cognitive health and relief from anxiety, stressful or depressive type conditions. Good for anxiety and upcoming stressful occasions.

Thuja, excellent remedy for warts, cysts and conditions of the womb.

Thymus Liq, very important as an immune booster for children and pre winter immunity enhancing remedy especially for the elderly

Vermex, use about 3 times per year as an essential wormer. If you keep pets use also for the pets.

Vir, mothers medicine chest remedy for when those winter viral infections occur. Use for adults and children

Essential Oils

Chamomile, is a good soothing oil and can help ease headaches and period pains. It is also a mood calmer. It helps to relieve inflamed itchy skin. If added to a cool bath, it is very soothing for sunburn.

Clary Sage, good to help with menstrual and menopausal problems as it has an oestrogenic effect. It can also help with postnatal depression. It is useful as a beauty aid as it helps to clear dandruff and helps oily hair.

Essential Oils, can ease skin problems and help heal wounds, bruises and dry itchy skin.

Evening Primrose Oil, it is good for relieving symptoms such as bloating and mood swings.

Geranium, is excellent for problematic skin and can be used to help dry or oily types. It can also help with eczema and shingles. It has a mood-lifting effect. It can help with mood swings and PMS.

Lavender, is one of a selected group of essential oils known as an adaptogen, which means it adapts to suit the body's needs. It is excellent for headaches and stress and can be applied directly to the temple. It is also good for spots, cuts and stings and can be applied neat. It can help to induce sleep or revive senses when exhausted.

Lemon, is the perfect aid for clear thinking and mental fatigue. Put a few drops into your shower gel to wake you up in the mornings.

Olive, comes to us from biblical times when the robbers attacked a man on the road to Jerrico. His saviour poured oil to heal his wounds. Today it is recognised as a food but can be used medicinally for a variety of conditions such as joint pain, bone health, cysts, lumps and inflammation.

Peppermint, is another good all-rounder. Place a few drops on a tissue, inhale and it can benefit the digestive system.

Rosemary, a versatile oil which is good for health and beauty. It has a powerful effect on the mind and can help concentration and relieve mental tiredness. Good for digestion and can improve the condition of hair.

Rosewood, good for the female reproductive system and can help with menstrual problems, menopausal symptoms and PMS. It is good to burn and enhance romance and is also good for skin when added to lotions. It improves appearance of skin tone and broken veins.

Sunflower Oil, is good in the morning on an empty stomach, take a tablespoon orally, swish around for 20 seconds, spit out and rinse the mouth. This helps to draw toxins out of the body.

Tea Tree Oil, has antiseptic healing properties. It is ideal for dabbing on cuts and spots, athletes foot, thrush, cold sores, verruca and warts. Burning the oil helps prevent infections being passed through the air and it also lifts the spirits. It also has strong antiseptic and antibacterial qualities. It can be used neat. It is a good natural way to repel insects. Adding tea tree to shampoo helps with hair care problems such as dandruff and head lice.

Ylang Ylang, can be used as a perfume or it can be burnt to lift the mood and create a romantic atmosphere. It can have a sedative effect which can help stress and sleepless-ness. It should however be used sparingly.

Nutrients

Vitamin A - essential to prevent mouth ulcers, poor night vision, acne, dry flaky skin, frequent colds or infections, dandruff, thrush or cystitis, diarrhoea.

B Complex Vitamins help to sustain and support the nervous system and support cognitive health.

Beta Carotene, helps protect against cell damage. Found in fruit and vegetables.

Biotin, deficiency can cause dry skin and scalp, poor hair condition, brittle nails, nausea and poor appetite.

Calcium, essential to prevent muscle cramps and tremors, brittle nails, tooth decay, high blood pressure and insomnia. It helps in the development of blood cells. Calcium is found in dairy products, eggs and green leafy vegetables.
A good home source is Egg Shells – ¼ teaspoon daily. Dry out shells in oven or open air then crush to dry matter. Sprinkle over salad or main meal.

To absorb calcium adequately your body must have an adequate store of magnesium. So adequate magnesium levels are crucial. Another problem for calcium uptake is the high levels of phosphate in the modern diet. Calcium metabolism is controlled by phosphate so the excess phosphate prevents uptake which can lead to other problems such as bone weakening or osteoporosis.

Home remedy for calcium is to collect egg shells from scrambled eggs or baking. Allow shells to dry, place in bowl, use mortar to grind up shell into to fine powder. Sprinkle on food / use in cooking or baking for a calcium and sulphur boost. A Blender or Food Processor can also be used to achieve the desired powder consistency.

Chromium, deficiency will cause craving for sweet foods, dizziness after long time without food, excessive thirst, cold sweats, daytime drowsiness, cold hands and feet. Chromium is essential for healthy adrenal function which is essential for vitality. It is also important for the pancreas assisting it with insulin production and for healthy thyroid function.

Cobalt, can lead to diminished levels of oxygen in the body. It is found in commercial cleaners and washing powder. There is also cobalt in dentures.

Epsom salts, were first discovered from the salt mines in Epson, UK. Theses salts are rich in magnesium and this mineral is central to good health. Magnesium deficiency can be caused by alcoholism, severe diarrhoea, or malnutrition. Excess calcium can deplete magnesium levels.

For home use, you can simply soak your feet in a basin of water and a half cup of Epsom salts. Alternatively have a relaxing bath which helps with stress relief and toxins flush.

Folic Acid, an important supplement to combat anaemia, fatigue, depression, poor appetite, forgetfulness, eczema, irritability. Essential nutrient during pregnancy to prevent neural tube defects.

Gelsemium, very important for the health of the pancreas.

Iron, deficiency will cause anaemia, fatigue, sore tongue, nausea, listlessness. Excess Iron may result in hemochromatosis which is a disorder of the blood.

Iodine, an important mineral for brain function and it is particularly important for healthy thyroid. Deficiency of iodine will cause developmental problems in the foetus and in early childhood. Seaweed is a good source.

Iron Phosphate, is good for sore throats.

Magnesium, one of the most important minerals for relief of high blood pressure, muscle cramps and tremors, headache, constipation, menstrual cramps, PMS, thyroid function, brain fatigue and prevention of depression.

It also helps with highly active children, strengthens bones, and helps with ME. Apricots are a good source of magnesium as well as being a pleasant fruit to eat. Consider magnesium as essential for all key organs and their function.

Magnesium phosphate, is good in cases of ME.

Manganese, use for muscle twitches, 'childhood 'growing pains, sore knee, dizziness, poor balance, blood sugar imbalance and improved vision.

Niacin B3, good to increase blood supply, spotting on skin, deficiencies, coated tongue, unpleasant mouth odour, sores, ulcers, tension, irritability, ear infections.

Platinium, essential for heart health especially the Aorta.

Potassium, important for muscle spasm.

Procydin, from Black Cherry, good for gout and relief of uric acid.

Sanguinaria, or bloodroot, is very useful for hot flushes, weak joints, hoarseness and sore throat.

Selenium, deficiencies can cause signs of premature aging, frequent infections and high blood pressure. Essential for healthy brain, adrenals and pancreas.

Sulphur, good nutrient for control of viral infection and brain function.

Vitamin A, which is Carotene converted by the body into Vitamin A. It helps with eye sight, and skin growth. Deficiency can cause frequent infections, especially of the upper respiratory tract, goose pimples appearing on skin, mouth ulcers, night blindness, dry and flaky skin. It's found in liver, butter, cheese and eggs.

Vitamin B – a group of vitamins which if taken in small amounts can help to release energy from food and promotes cell development and good mental health. Sources include brown rice, peas, beans, cereals, dairy products as well as green leafy vegetables, meat, poultry and eggs. A daily good quality B Group Supplement helps prevent many chronic conditions.

The B group of Vitamins consists of the following;

- **B1**, a deficiency will result in tender muscles, pins and needles, fatigue, eye pains, stomach pain, constipation, poor concentration and memory.
- **B2** helpful for cracked lips on corner of mouth, split nails, itchy eyes, sensitivity to light, inflamed tongue. Deficiency can cause cataracts, eczema, burning eyes, cracked lips.
- **B3**, deficiency can cause acne, dermatitis, anxiety or tension, diarrhoea, insomnia, irritability, poor memory, headaches or migraines, bleeding gums and lack of energy.
- **B5**, deficiency can cause fatigue, listlessness, poor concentration, memory loss, burning feet, tension and anxiety, muscle tremors and cramps, teeth grinding.
- **B6**, deficiency can cause water retention, irritability, depression or nervousness, flaky skin, cracked lips or tongue.
- **B12**, can cause pale skin, eczema, dermatitis irritability, tension and anxiety, pins and needles, constipation, memory loss and confusion. Good food sources are cheese, eggs and barley.

Vitamin C, found in fruit, vegetables and potatoes helps fight infections. Deficiency results in more frequent colds and other infections, such as wounds hard to heal, bleeding gums, nose bleeds, easy bruising, red pimples on skin.

Vitamin D, helps to produce healthy skin, bones and teeth and maintain good cognitive health. Very important in cases of ADD and ADHD or autism in children, also important in pregnancy for the health of mother and baby. Natural source is sunshine. Half hour each day with face and arms exposed will be sufficient. However that will be difficult to achieve in winter so supplements will be necessary.

Food sources are mackerel, eggs and milk. Deficiency will result in poor skin condition, tooth decay, hair loss, excessive sweating, depression, muscle spasms and rickets.

Vitamin E, helps to promote healthy bones and teeth. It is found in wholemeal bread and green leafy vegetables. Deficiency can result in infertility, low sex drive, exhaustion after exercise, varicose veins and loss of muscle tone.

Zinc, deficiency is noted by white flecks on the finger nails, acne or greasy pale skin, stretch marks, loss of appetite, tendency to depression, frequent infections, low immunity. Poor sense of smell and taste may also be signs of deficiency. Zinc is perhaps the most critical nutrient for mental health especially condition like ADHD and autism. Very important for hormonal health, including PMS and memopause. Use also for viral infections such as herpes and EBV. Good sources of zinc include oysters, nuts, seeds and fish.

Vital Nutrients for children

- Vitamin A helps with eyesight, skin and growth. Found in liver, butter, cheese and eggs.
- Beta Carotene helps to protect against cell damage, found in fruit and vegetables.
- Vitamins B1, B2, B12 help to release energy from food and promote cell development. Found in brown rice, peas, beans, cereals, dairy products, leafy green vegetables, meat, poultry and eggs.

Chapter Seven

Energy Medicine

Energy Medicine Therapies

Energetic medicine therapies are an essential ingredient in any natural health practice. This will include home-opathy, kinesiology, bio resonance, reiki, reflexology iridology, colour therapy and acupuncture. From my own perspective, homeopathy, kinesiology, bio resonance and nutrition have been the key elements in my practice from almost the beginning. In so far as foods are concerned, I encourage clients to maximise their efforts by obtaining nutrients through ordinary food rather than supplements.
In addition, I encourage private practices such as prayer, yoga, meditation, reflex-ology and exercise, all of which I consider to be spiritual nutrition.

Reflexology

Research shows that hand and foot reflexology originated in ancient Egypt. This fact is evidenced by inscriptions found in a physician's tomb (Mastaba). Whether these methods were the exact same as practiced today is still uncertain. However, in my opinion the similarities between the two are very close indeed.

• **Doctor William H. Fitzgerald** was probably the leading person involved in this form of medicine at the beginning of the 20th Century. On April 29th 1934, it was reported at a dinner party that the singer's upper register tones were flat and throat surgeons were unable to help. On examining her feet, Dr. Fitzgerald advised the singer that the issue was caused by a callus on her right big toe. By manipulating her feet's pressure points, as is the art of reflexology, the entertainer was able to sing two tones higher than ever before. This was within twenty min-utes of the consultation.

• Another expert in the reflexology service of this century was **Eunice D. Ingham Stopfel**, (1889 - 1974). It is this lady who is credited with the rebirth of reflexology and through her encouragement, it is where we know it today. It's from the work of her nephew, **Dwight C. Byers***, that most of my deeper understanding comes from.

What is Reflexology?

Reflexology is a science that works on the principle that there are reflex areas in the feet and hands, which correspond to all of the glands, organs, and parts of the body.

---

* **Better Health with Foot Reflexology** - *Dwight C. Byers Ingham Publishing 2001, ISBN 1891130005*

It is a unique method of using the thumb and fingers on these reflex areas of the foot and hand:

- Relieve stress and tension.
- Improve blood supply and promote the unblocking of nerve impulses.
- Help nature achieve homeostasis.

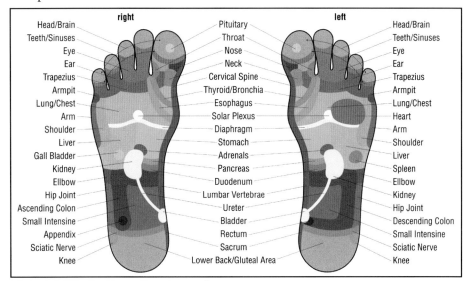

source: iStock.com/PeterHermesFurian

Essentially, reflexology is the art of *fine tuning* the body by accessing its energy pathways. I would love to see and strongly recommend that Hospitals and Nursing Homes use reflexology for their patients as an alternative to drugs and sedatives. An evening session of reflexology or a back massage would be very relaxing for an elderly person or for any age. After a session, they are more likely to get a restful sleep without the aid of drugs.

Individual Cases

Ceoladh was 7 years old in the summer of 1987. She had been suffering from a loss of feeling in both legs for many weeks. This deterioration was progressive, she made her First Communion with the aid of crutches.

Her family was incredibly concerned. Ceoladh spent three weeks in hospital, but despite extensive tests, she was discharged without a diagnosis.

Within ten minutes of working on Ceoladh's feet, I could ascertain that her lymphatic system had been compromised and in turn had affected her nervous system, thus causing the lack of feeling in her legs. After the first treatment, she begun to feel her limbs become more supple. By the second treatment, the sensation in her legs had begun to improve and within eight weeks Ceoladh had fully recovered.

Ceoladh and her family were introduced through her experience to reflexology as a wonderful healing modality and many years later continue to incorporate this holistic approach to all aspects of life.

Maura was 38 and thought she was going through an early menopause. Her GP decided to check her hormone levels. Results suggested she was menopausal as she had not had a period for two years and suffered hot and cold sweats.

On visiting my clinic, I noted a very congested lymphatic system and I recommended an intensive detoxification of hot sea salt baths and body brushing. She also did two months daily manual lymphatic drainage. I also noted congestion and inflammation around her ovaries. I concentrated on this using massage and reflexology. I also gave her exercises to do for her ovaries. She committed to regular herbal tonics, liver flushes and a plain diet which excluded coffee and alcohol. Three months later she was feeling fantastic and by six months her periods returned to normal. I also recommended black strap molasses and an immune booster.

Bio Resonance Therapy

EAV stands for **Electro-Acupuncture** according to **Voll**. Dr. Reinhold Voll (1909-1989) was a German Physician who initiated the application of electronic technology to the Chinese system of traditional acupuncture. Voll, an architect by profession, developed cancer, fought the condition and recovered his health. Thereafter he studied medicine and became a doctor. In the 1950s, he surveyed acupuncture points and the related meridians using a standard Ohmmeter. This was a routine electrical measurement tool of the time, but from it developed the science of *electro-acupuncture – EAV*. Dr Voll developed a device called Dermatron, with which he was able to establish a connection between a medicinal product and an organ by pressing a metal probe on the meridian which related to that particular organ.

Dr. Helmut W. Schimmel (1929-) is a German doctor who devised a simpler method of diagnostics, again using resonant procedures. He created a circuit by having the patient hold an electrode (metal tube) in one hand whilst he placed a metal point probe (a small object similar to a writing pen) against a single acupuncture point. This produced a signal, which was a reflection of the energetic flow or health of the organ represented by the acupuncture point. Schimmel inserted ampules containing homeopathic remedies into the circuit which resulted in an alteration to the output signal. Schimmel named this the Vegetative Reflects Test (V.R.T later renamed Vega). Using this technique, he established a relationship between the homeopathic remedy and the particular organs and in fact from this process he developed a range of products which he described as *Resonance Homeopathy.*

These remedies were combination preparations containing at least three starting materials at low potencies, similar to many remedies available today. Further research indicated a resonance relationship with various single homeopathic preparations. The experience gained from this form of testing validated the concept of homeopathic resonance and confirmed the belief long held by energy practitioners that homeopathic medications worked by matching, now described as *resonating with its target*. The target could be an organ, a group of cells, or the person as a whole, in fact, any living organism, plant or animal. This is why homeopathic therapy is so versatile. Specific remedies can be prepared for viral, bacterial or other pathological conditions, or for any physiological or bodily malfunction.

Homeopathy

Homeopathy has more than a 200-year history of use as a safe and efficacious form of medicine. It has been used extensively in central European countries, notably Germany, Austria and France for most of that period. German immigrants to the United States introduced homeopathy to their new homeland and in fact it became very popular and extensively used there until the end of the 19th Century. The advent of *scientific medicine* backed by powerful and wealthy investors resulted in private funding almost drying up, which was a near fatal blow to homeopathy. Committed doctors and patients alike kept it alive and active. Over the last 30 years, its popularity has been on the increase in many countries including Member States of the EU. Outside of Europe, it is also widely used in India, Argentina and Brazil.

The founding father of modern homeopathy is Samuel Hahnemann, a German physician, pharmacist, scientist, writer and translator. Hahnemann had become disillusioned with conventional medical practices so he left practice to give time to healing research. He funded himself as a lecturer and translator during this time. He experimented with the concept of *similars*, an oft discussed but unproven method of treatment. He found that Cinchona, then used to treat malaria, would cause symptoms similar to those of malaria in a healthy person. Further tests with other commodities yielded similar outcomes. This he described as the *Law of Similars*.

source: iStock.com/stocksnapper

123

His experimentation also consisted of diluting the dosage level of then existing medicinal compounds so as to establish at what point or level of dosage he could achieve a successful outcome. As he prepared his mixtures, he gave each a vigorous shaking and to his surprise, the more he diluted, the more effective the outcome. He went on to discover that the vigorous shaking dynamized the solution and Hahnemann concluded that it was this energized feature which gave the compound added curative properties. Today, the dynamisation process is referred to as *potentization*. Hahnemann went on to develop a mathematical model which became the foundation stone of his new and innovative medicine, now referred to as a *serial dilution and succussion* (the shaking process). He developed the basis of a new healing system which he named **Homeopathy,** as he was keen to differentiate it from Allopathy, ie the term used for conventional or chemical medicine.

He added other features to his new medicine, chief of which was *the minimum dose.* He was strong in his insistence that the organism needed only minimum stimulation to activate its *vital force.* Allopathy at that time was driven by high-dose pharmacology, both single and mixtures of compounds.

He activated the concept of *miasms,* with a number of sub-categories. His miasmatic theories included Syphilitic, Sycotic and Psoric. These he described as features of the human condition resulting from inheritance, genetics or prevailing conditions of life and circumstances. In modern times, we could add a number of conditions such as AIDs and electromagnetic stress. In future decades or generations, we will see a new miasm for the current addiction to social media. Miasm comes from the Greek *miasma,* meaning taint or fault.

Through its use in clinical practice and an increasing level of scientific evaluation, we have a greater understanding of homeopathy today, with more information available on how it meets the needs of many people and its wide spectrum of uses.

- It can aid everyday ailments such as prevention or remedial action for the common cold, flu, coughs, hay fever, sensitivities, sinusitis and excess mucous.
- It can be used topically for bruising, scarring, joint stiffness, aches and wound healing.
- It is very effective for female conditions such as hormonal imbalances, menopause, PMS and the endocrine malfunctions.

- It can be used effectively to help produce digestive enzymes, encourage digestion and absorption and enhance body chemistry.
- It is very effective in the control of pathogens such as bacteria, viruses, fungal overgrowth and parasites.
- As a preventative medicine, it can be used to enhance detoxification of heavy metals, chemicals and pesticides and so prevent toxic build-up and onset of illness.
- As a safe, effective medicine, it is ideal for children and young adults. In the case of infants, it can also be applied topically because of its energetic properties.
- It can be used preventively to boost immunity, enhance organ function, provide energy and vitality, promote optimum health and prevent minor or serious adverse health conditions.
- It can be used emotionally to lift spirits, relieve low moods, enhance cogninive function and assist in times of distress such as family illness, loss or bereavement.
- It promotes healthy ageing as it is extremely safe and gentle in its application.
- It integrates positively with other natural health therapies and supplements.
- Doctors recommend homeopathy as a safe and reliable alternative to antibiotics.*
- It can be used alongside conventional treatments and medications including drugs and surgery.**
- Homeopathy is very effective throughout the care of animals, offering an equally-wide variety of health applications.

Kinesiology

Dr. George Goodheart (1918-2008) was an American Chiropractor who combined his knowledge and experience of biology with his knowledge of the ancient Chinese art of acupuncture and the meridian system. Dr. Goodheart found that when evaluating the energy flow, the muscles of the body responded to stimuli. For example - if he introduced a helpful herb or vitamin, the muscle tested strongly. On the contrary, if he introduced a toxic compound to the person's energy field, such as a chemical, the muscle would go weak.

---

* **Homeopathy: The Effective Alternative To Antibiotics** - *By Dr. Mukesh Batra, Townsend Letter: July 2013*
** **Cancer and Homeopathy.** - *Dr Jean-Lionel Bagot. Unimedica, Narayana Verlang Nlumenplatz 2 D-79400 Kandern Germany*

He carried out extensive research into the role of muscle responses as part of biological processes and founded a new method of non-verbal evaluation which he named *Applied Kinesiology*, derived from the Greek *kinesis*, to move.

Goodheart's research covered all types of medicines, nutrients, herbs and homeopathy. This was a further example of resonance, the energetic pattern of a remedy matching the energetic flow of the patient – frequency matching. For homeopathy, it had another advantage. It could facilitate the calculation of exactly what the body calls for, *the minimum dose*. Hahnemann's rule was observed through communication with the sub-conscious mind.

Kinesiology has become a prominent form of measurement and evaluation and its popularity is growing worldwide. It was scientifically validated by a number of scientists in the decades since Goodheart who brought it into the public mind. Dr. John Diamond, a psychiatrist, used kinesiology to determine the hidden determinants of human behaviour and the impact on an individual's health resulting from such feelings as desires, likes, dislikes, feelings, attitudes and behaviour. Dr. David Hawkins, also a psychiatrist, used Kinesiology in his clinic. He conducted thousands of tests on individuals, groups, communities, sectors and public figures in politics, arts and sport to determine various levels of consciousness. He drew direct parallels between personal behaviour, wellbeing and health of individuals with that of community, social class, profession, occupation or society as a whole. In homeopathic terms, Dr. Hawkins was validating Hahnemann's view, expressed through *beschaffenheit*, that the individual was reflective of his total environment and it manifested in his state of health. Through the new science of *Epigenetics*, scientists now tell us that we don't just belong to our genes and ancestors but we are also formed by our environment.*

Emotional Freedom Techniques (EFT)

EFT, also referred to as tapping, is an ideal home or workplace procedure to relieve tension or stress and bring about a relaxing state. Tapping lightly with the finger tips on key energy points causes positive energy to flow through the meridians and energise key organs and glands that control the relevant emotions. EFT works on the same principle as Acupressure or Reflexology which has been explained earlier. The great advantage is that a person can perform it on themselves at any time.

---

* **The Biology of Belief** - *Bruce H. Lipton , Ph. D. Mountain of love productions ISBN 0-9759914-7-7*

The procedure is as follows:

1. Use four fingers to tap the Crown, say 15 or 20 times in each session of EFT that you undertake. Use reasonably rapid light taps.
2. Repeat the gentle but firm tapping action above both eyes.
3. Follow the tapping along the hairline to the top of each temple.
4. Follow that with taps directly over both upper cheek bones.
5. Then repeat directly on the upper lip.
6. Followed by direct tapping on the chin.
7. Fingers then move to the shoulder where you tap on the collar bone.
8. The last tapping is in the armpit on each side, left hand to right armpit and visa versa.

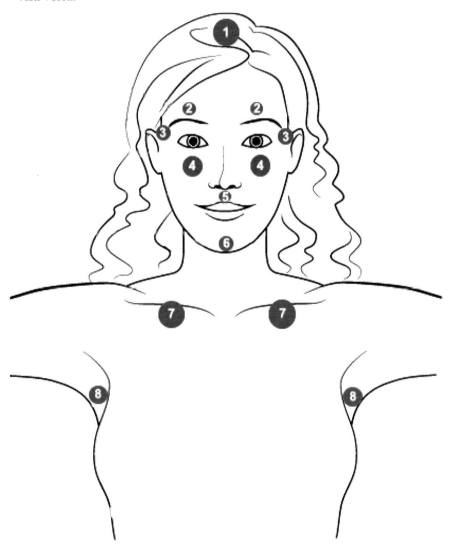

Flower Therapy

Dr. Edward Bach (1886-1936) was the innovator and founder of Flower Therapy which bears his name in the range of products marketed as Bach Flower Remedies. Bach trained as a doctor and worked in different hospitals in the United Kingdom in his early years. He studied homeopathy and started to practice classically full time. He developed a tumour on his spleen which was removed surgically. Doctors said he would only live for three months. However he lived for a further fourteen years. During that time he researched a new method of healing alongside his homeopathic practice. His theory was that the energy of flowers could resonate with human emotions and provide healing. Could he do this without harvesting and processing the plants as used in homeopathy? His aim was to use *flower healing* with the minimum amount of processing. He initially collected the dew drops in the morning which he then preserved in brandy. As that was a slow process, he developed a method of holding the flower over a bowl of spring water and letting the sun shine through. Bach believed this process transferred the energy of the flower to the water. The water was then preserved in brandy.

Good mental and emotional health is critical to overall wellbeing and quality of life and for this purpose Flower Therapy is widely used for emotional healing. Different brands have been developed by individual companies and each with a unique philosophy and healing application. The best known, apart from Bach Flowers would be Australian Bush Flower Essences developed by Ian White which are now available in many countries.

Colour Therapy

Everyone loves a splash of colour to liven up their day. They look forward to the change of seasons so they can wear brighter colours and reflect the brilliance of nature around them. Colour Therapy is an ancient, holistic art which was used to aid wellbeing and health maintenance.

Many people will have heard of the ancient Colour Temples of Egypt and Greece. Whilst modern use is largely provided for its complementary role, throughout history, colour therapy played a significant part in traditional healing.

In energy medicine, we look at vibrations and frequencies. All atoms in the universe possess energy and resonate at their own individual forces. Within the body, all organs, glands and body systems have their own vibrational energies. Different colours will have their frequency which can harmonise with matching frequency in the body, which in turn harmonises with universal frequencies. For example, the light wave of any colour will pass through the eyes, stimulate the pineal gland and feed into the Limbic area of the brain. It will pass to the pituitary gland (the master gland) which will in turn stimulate the gland which resonates with that colour. This harmonising can have a positive impact on emotional and mental wellbeing. Some examples of colours and their impact on organs, body function and health conditions influenced are:

Colour	Organ/Function	Health Condition
Yellow	Motor and Sensory. Lymphatic, Nervous System, Bones.	Stimulates motor and nervous system, lowers melancholy states, promotes bile and pancreatic juices, assists with diabetes.
Red	Blood and Nervous System.	Improves circulation, liver, assists detox and promotes sight, smell and taste.
Orange	Stomach, Lungs and Bones.	Stimulates lungs and thyroid. Activates stomach glands and promotes enzyme production. Promotes calcium absorption and therefore helps bone strength.
Green	Heart and Limbic.	Helps with heart health, blood clots, acts as pituitary stimulant and as detox for mycotoxins.
Blue	Throat and Limbic.	Stimulates the pineal gland, improves vitality. Helps with colds and sore throat.
Lemon	Thymus, Immune and Muscular System.	Acts as stimulant, relieves congestion in lungs and bronchia and good for bone health.
Magenta	Heart, Kidneys and Adrenals.	Makes you feel good, lifts your Aura. Puts pep in your step.

A good idea for general use would be to wear colourful clothes suitable for what you are doing and geared towards what you want to achieve. It is a long established practice, to wear green on St. Patrick's Day or wear County or Club colours on match day. It is so important to have intent and feel intent, throughout your day, such as at work, in school and within your life. It is vital; it sets you up and gets your mind into the essential framework required for success.

If on any morning your heart is feeling uneasy or misses a beat, then wear a green top, jacket or cardigan. You could also wear green socks to enhance circulation. After some experience of this practice you will begin to notice the benefit. The same approach would apply if your throat is raw and your voice crackling. Wear a blue scarf around your neck with a blue top. Note the improvement soon after. If your baby daughter is uneasy and tearful, provided you are happy there is no serious condition, dress her in pink or place a pink shawl around her.

Music in itself is also a great therapy. Music and colour combined is even better. Use this combination whenever you can. Listen to classical or church music as both can be helpful. They have both been developed over the centuries by Masters of their Art.

The Chakras

Throughout energy medicine, we discuss energy points or energy wheels to describe the manner in which the body manages itself through channels to communicate with its wider environment. This being the daily interaction with people, places, community, work, society, planet and the universe in which we live.

We are all connected and interdependent. We need each other, we are dependent on each other. If we hurt one another, we ultimately hurt ourselves. So, it is important to understand how we relate to this wider environment of which we are part of.

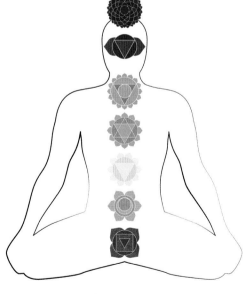

source: iStock.com/PeterHermesFurian

To help us with this challenge, body is equipped with seven key energy points which scientists can now measure as exhibiting greater levels of energy or vibration at those specific points. These points have specific roles to help us connect and harmonise our inward feeling and desires with our outward connections.

The chakras are as follows:

Chakra	Associated Organs/Glands	Associated Colour	Purpose
1st Chakra **Root**	Rectum, Tailbone, Sex Organs	Red	Keeps us grounded and is our connection with the earth, our source of energy and life.
2nd Chakra **Sacral**	Spleen, Ovaries, Urinary tract, Uterus, Kidneys and Adrenals	Orange	Is associated with feelings, flow, freedom, sexuality, passion, vitality and zest for life.
3rd Chakra **Solar Plexus**	Liver, Pancreas, Stomach, Small intestine	Yellow	Reflects our personal strength and courage to take on and complete challenges, overcome difficulties and obstacles that we encounter.
4th Chakra **Heart**	Heart, Thymus, Lungs, Lymph, Immune system	Green	Enables us to connect with and help others including the skills development to differentiate empathy from sympathy.
5th Chakra **Throat**	Thyroid, Parathyroid, Neck, Ears, and Respiratory System	Blue	Our communication centre which enables us to issue and receive messages and assimilate those messages in a beneficial manner.
6th Chakra **Brow**	Limbic System, Pituitary, Hypothalamus, Autonomic Nervous System and Eyes	Purple	Also known as the third eye, the brow chakra provides guidance and regulates the lower five chakras. So it is our centre of wisdom. Crucial therefore that it is in balance as it is our communicator with ourselves.
7th Chakra **Crown**	Pineal gland and Central Nervous System, Head and Hair	White	Our connection with the Creator, with God that guides us and the Universe that sustains us.

Meditation, Mindfulness and Yoga

Meditation is a very important exercise as part of health and wellbeing. It is grounding, relaxing and health enhancing. I recommend it as an everyday practice, especially for people who are in stressful situations at work, must comply with output schedules or travel extensively. However, its benefits equally apply to any person in family and community life as an antidote to stress. Meditation is an ancient custom which has been widely used, especially in Eastern cultures, on a continuous basis. In western cultures, it was replaced by Church or Religious practices for a significant part of the last two centuries. It is growing in popularity again as people come to know of its special benefits.

Meditation styles can vary from person to person. Essentially, it is your own ability to make yourself still for a period of time. You should focus and quieten your mind for intervals of fifteen minutes twice daily. However, it can be as few as two minutes or as many as thirty, as you wish. Stilling the mind for a short period is very therapeutic. Block out your worries and anxieties of the day and relax. You will feel the benefits after a few sessions. You could also practice a chakra meditation. Go through each of the seven chakras one by one, allowing a minute or more to connect with each energy wheel, concentrating on how its free-flowing energy can benefit your wellness. Notice how your body moves with each inhalation and exhalation.

I recommend visiting local group meditations within your locality. It is now widely available. It is very comforting and healing to share with other people. Meditation is like mass, a concert or a seminar; it is the sharing of something special.

Mindfulness is essentially another form of meditation, focusing on a special topic in a thoughtful meditative manner. However, it is meant to help you be aware and be in the present, to be alive and mindful of what and where you are. It is intended to help in particular situations so as to respond appropriately, rather than react in a defensive manner, which can be stressful. However, it is not about pleasing or being nice, it is about being appropriate in the circumstances.

Yoga is yet another form of energy medicine where you utilise special postures and practices as part of your relaxing regime. Yoga is taken from antiquity and there have been many different art forms developed over the centuries. Before undertaking yoga, I recommend you attend a course with a suitable trainer. There are different providers. For beginners, athletes, sports specialists, businessmen and businesswomen, yoga for cancer patients and so on. Like exercise, select the course that is best for you.

Chapter Eight

Case Histories

Autism and ASD
Antoni Simovic

My daughter Natalia was born on 6th March 2000, the third of 4 children for Aine and myself. Natalia was born by caesarean section but otherwise the birth was normal. She grew up in our family home in Citluk, Bosnia and Herzegovina. For the first 2 years of her life Natalia was a normal child with healthy development just like our other 3 children.

Three months after her 2nd birthday she was given the MMR child vaccination, which was standard practice in our area. Unlike our other children Natalia started to react badly soon after. She became withdrawn with strange actions like running away from people and walking on her toes. From there on she had a very poor level of progress with words and speech development, visual connection with people, and abnormal interaction with parents and siblings. At times, she would seem full of energy but at the same time could be extremely disturbed. Immediately we took her for assessment where autistic disorder

Antoni and Natalia 2017

was mentioned. One Doctor stated a bad batch of vaccine had been received from the UN as a number of children in the area had been affected in a similar manner. Soon after, the UN published in the local newspaper, that they did not donate any vaccines to Bosnia and Herzegovina that year.

After receiving the diagnosis in Mostar we went to a special clinic in America where the same diagnosis was confirmed. At a further examination at a Medical Centre at the University of Sarajevo, when Natalia was 6 years old, the Doctor noted that she was particularly motor restless in unfamiliar environments. She would scream, her voice was inarticulate; she paid little attention to her parents and would run aimlessly around the room and along the corridor. It was noted that she had a distinct possibility of hurting herself. Frequently she would put her hands over her ears and appeared visibly upset and frightened. According to the doctor's opinion this was Autistic Disorder.

Further treatment

At the age of 7 Natalia was evaluated by Dr Cindy Schneider, MD. At this point she has been on Abilify 5 mg daily for 1 year. No effective response had yet been seen from this medication. She was then prescribed a range of supplements.

It was also recommended that she receives food allergy testing, plasma, urinary, amino acid and other laboratory tests. The results found that she had high amounts of 9 different heavy metals in her system, including: lead, mercury, cadmium, nickel, etc.

My wife Aine had recognised that medical practice in our country did not cater for such problems in children. Aine had grown up in Ireland and after school she joined the Garda. She worked as a Ban Garda for 10 years and then decided to take leave to do some voluntary work. She joined the Pilgrimage Centre at Medjugorje as a Pilgrim Organiser for one year. We met there and later married so Bosnia became home to Aine. During this time she worked as a volunteer helping people who were displaced during the Civil War.

During these times, we were desperately seeking a treatment that would help our daughter. Aine spoke to a Nun, a religious Sister from Bosnia and Herzegovina, who had some experience with health conditions like Natalia experienced. The Nun came to visit us in Mostar, but when she saw the public health conditions and the manner in which the children were frequently restrained, effectively caged, she did not want to participate any further. The Nun recommended she speak to Sr Lydwina Farrell from Ireland, who was a member of a society which helped children with behavioural and cognitive disorders. Sr Lydwina stated that the best person she could recommend was a Naturopath near Dublin named Agnes McGuinness.

It was comforting for Aine to have the Irish connection but whilst it was very difficult financially we made our way to Dublin. We packed our car and drove to the North of France, where we boarded our ferry. The ferry ride was unbearable and nerve-wracking. Natalia, who was 9 at the time, was restless during the whole trip. Soon after we set sail, the captain of the ship came with the ship's medic, insisting to sedate her since a lot of people were complaining. We refused the sedation, and spent the whole night comforting her. From Rosslare, we went straight to Agnes. Sr Lydwina was present for the first consultation. Natalia was in a particularly bad state on the first day and I had to physically hold her so that Agnes could perform the tests that she normally carries out. I had not seen those skills or procedures previously. It was called Bio Energy Testing and later I came to know about Kinesiology.

I told Agnes about the bad batch of vaccine. She said it could be excess mercury in the batch or even the aluminium content. Agnes offered another comment that applies to many children. Their immune system is so weak at the time of vaccination that they are unable to handle the shock that goes with it and their tiny bodies are unable to detoxify the toxic metal associated with the vaccine.

She said mercury is typically used as a preservative for the vaccine, so now I understood that the vaccine in itself might be good but it was the added mercury or aluminium which is the issue. Those metals are a very toxic material and a problem for neurological and cognitive development.

Agnes recommended several practical measures to help Natalia in her education and ordinary living. This excluded many items from the diet, specifically products with high sugar content, like fizzy drinks and sweets. Foods high in sugar and foods containing high levels of phosphorous should be excluded. She also recommended a number of homeopathic remedies like Mag Phos for brain development, Abies Nigra and Digestive Enzyme for gastric problems. Adrenal Liq to help with the sympathetic nervous system and address Natalia's low adrenal readings. She provided Vir for viral infections and Sleep Ease to help her relax. Omega fish oil was recommended for cognitive and brain function.
I noted that within 3 days Natalia had calmed and the journey home was much better than the journey inwards.

Since the first visit to Agnes, Natalia has made fantastic progress and I wish my wife was here to see it. Sadly we lost Aine with her death in 2011. In 2010 she was diagnosed with bowel cancer. Later she had a blood disorder involving the Haemoglobin. As a teenager, she had a car accident, as a result she had a metal plate to stabilise her back. Our four children were born by caesarean section. Then for the last 3 years of her life she blamed herself for having Natalia vaccinated in childhood which stressed her terribly. In her last year, apart from the cancer and blood problems she was suffering from exhaustion and burnout. Despite the loss I was pleased that she had seen a big improvement in Natalia for a year before her death.

This year June 2017, is our fourth visit without Aine and our sixth visit altogether to Agnes. Natalia has been attending school continuously. The teachers at her school are delighted with her progress and find her a pleasure to work with.

We continue to maintain the special dietary needs for Natalia and the homeopathic remedies and other supplements that have been recommended. I want to take this opportunity to thank all the parties who have helped our family in so many different ways. My special thanks go to Agnes McGuinness for the enormous contribution to Natalia's health, and the wellbeing of the rest of the family. In addition, her personal generosity has been tremendous.
Having visited Agnes 6 times, I can clearly see the services she has provided to thousands of people over 45 years.

I hope the authorities in Ireland and everywhere will recognise the importance of those special health services and promote them for the benefit of the many people who are suffering from new health conditions and others harmed by medical practice.

Natalia, Antoni and Angnes in Clonalvy

Antoni Simovic 28th June 2017, Krehin Gradac, Citluk, Bosnia-Herzegovina. Email. antoni.simovic@gmail.com

Alopecia

During the summer (2012) I noticed a bald spot on my son's head. At the time my son was 3 years old and had a fine head of blonde curls. The bald spot was approximately 1cm in diameter. This sounds small but it was situated on the crown of his head where the hair parts naturally, so the bald spot was quite noticeable. I kept an eye on this bald spot over a number of weeks observing that it was totally bald and smooth with no signs of infection.

After a number of weeks, I visited my GP with my son. The GP diagnosed alopecia. Alopecia he told me was hair loss of unknown cause and that it was not related to any infection. There was no treatment. I also was told – it might clear up or could get worse.

About a month after this GP consultation I met Agnes and asked her about this problem. She looked at the spot, noted that there was no hair at all on the area and said *"yes, that's because his playing with dinkies"*. Agnes advised me not just to remove them from my son, but to make sure they were gone from the house. We duly collected them and got rid of them all. Within a few weeks, we could see the hair beginning to grow back and within 6 weeks or so the bald spot was completely gone and replaced by lovely blonde curls.

I should say that Agnes had never been in my house or seen my son's extensive collection of dinkies. My son asked occasionally about the dinkies but in a short time asked no more.

Bladder Tumour

Adrienne Druett

After many visits to the doctor due to occasional blood in my urine, in October 2014, I was referred to the hospital for a CT urinary tract scan, as a result I had a biopsy late November. The biopsy diagnosis was G3 TCC bladder with adenocarcinomatous differentiation a 2cm tumour in the dome of my bladder. This was explained by a Urology/Oncology Specialist nurse who stated that the treatment lies between a resection of the bladder tumour or indeed more radical treatment, which was overwhelming and I was emotionally very upset and my head was spinning trying to take it all in. Christmas of that year was not a joyous time for me.

Arrangements were made for me to visit Agnes early January 2015 which was the start of a wonderful recovery. On testing, Agnes found my immune system was run down and lacking in various Vitamins and Minerals. Agnes recommended I should take Magnesium Phosphate, Synergistic Zinc, Dandelion, Burdock Extract, Echinacea and Calcium (egg shells).

I was also to take Aloe Vera & Honey, Apple Cider Vinegar, Beetroot Juice, Crude Black Strap Molasses and Essiac Tea. I also had the Borna Virus for which I was given tablets and used the Borna programme on the RifeMedic daily together with the programmes for cancer, Bladder, Blood Cleanse, Circulation and various stimulation programmes. Agnes recommended which points to massage to help circulation and Lymphatic drainage. Tapping was advised to help with Circulation and the Adrenals.

It was recommended to detox the liver, bile, and kidney system and also do a parasite cleanse on a regular basis.

Since January 2015, I have visited Agnes every 8 to 10 weeks and a recent Flexible Cystoscopy shows the resection is clear. It was not easy as I had to spend many hours daily with all the treatments and many trips across the Irish Sea but the result makes it all worthwhile.

It is thanks to Agnes that one year after I was given what I thought was a death sentence, I am back to full health.

Adrienne Druett

Breast cancer
Rena Condrot

Christmas Eve 1997 arrived, it was a lovely morning and today I was bringing my nieces and nephews (all seven of them aged 3 - 8) to see Santa Claus as had been my custom for years past. I had been feeling a little tired from time to time however, I was 53 years of age and many people particularly the medical profession had said it was my age.

Three years earlier I had discovered a lump on my breast and undergone an operation for the removal of the breast and half of the lymph glands, and then had a course of chemotherapy following the operation.

Earlier in 1997 I had discovered another lump in the area and it too was removed and proved to be malignant. This time I received a course of radiation. By November my energy levels had not returned to the levels previously enjoyed. Having had a very enjoyable time in Dublin with the children we arrived home with seven very tired children ready for bed and looking forward to Christmas Day and the surprise that Santa would bring them. Sitting in bed that night I too was tired and once again noticed that pain had returned to the underarm. This pain I had on each occasion before lumps were previously discovered. I did a really thorough examination and was horrified to discover a tiny lump deep in the arm pit. Surely I thought the cancer could not have returned for a third time.

Christmas and the New Year were very difficult for me and had well passed before I could see my oncologist. He said the lump must be removed immediately. It was possibly malignant but we would have to wait on the laboratory reports. The laboratory reports arrived back and confirmed our worst fears. Once again, I had to have Chemotherapy. The Oncologist said it was absolutely essential and I had no choice but to go down this road. This time it would be more difficult, the medicine would be more severe and toxic, I would also lose my hair. I had been very ill and tired on the earlier course of Chemotherapy, I did not relish the forthcoming six months of treatment and the 18 months of recovery required.

My friends insisted that I visit Agnes McGuinness, a complementary medical practitioner who lived not too far away. Immediately Agnes put me on two machines the Valkion Oxygen Machine and the Valkion light/pain machine. I could feel that the machines were doing me good but had difficulty in quantifying the positive effects, however four weeks down the road after the second application of Chemotherapy it became very easy to quantify the very positive effects of the machines.

Chemotherapy had the effect of making me very nauseous, exhausted, low immunity to normal bacteria and viruses, the sensation that one's mind or brain is in a fog this progresses very quickly to the sensation that the brain is operating in a bucket of very thick glue. Whilst one's thought process remains reasonably good; the train of thought is easily lost and concentration ability is greatly reduced. It was also very difficult to perform simple tasks such as dialing a telephone number. Usually it took three attempts before getting the correct number. As a practicing accountant, it was very important to me that I maintain skills in numerics during my treatment.

I had experienced all of these problems on my previous course of chemotherapy therefore these problems were not new to me. Nor was the dreadful nauseous feeling new to me. As the treatment progressed I would have the sensation that my lungs were reduced to a quarter capacity therefore any type of physical activity would be very difficult.

Always when I was released from hospital after receiving Chemotherapy I would go straight to Agnes and use the machines. After the second Chemotherapy treatment, it became very clear that the machines seemed to 'clear' my system. My head would be very clear and I would get a terrific boost of energy. By the next morning, I would be back to very low energy levels, inability to concentrate for more than 10 minutes, reversing figures and the sensation that my brain was operating from a bucket of glue.

A visit to Agnes to use her machines would straighten me out for the day and give me the necessary energy boost. These were the immediate and most obvious benefits of the machines. I would never miss a day on the machines. As the treatment of Chemotherapy progressed I maintained the status quo and indeed towards the middle to last quarter of the treatment my energy level was going up. In the beginning, I was on very strong anti-sickness medication again as more chemotherapy was put into my body I was gradually getting milder anti sick medicine.

It is most interesting that by the time I had reached my last Chemotherapy treatment I did not need or take any anti sickness medicine, my mind was still very clear after using the machines each day.

The last time I had the sensation of 25% lung capacity, this time I did have the sensation of reduced lung capacity but it was minimal and felt as if I still had 80% lung capacity. I have continued to work throughout my treatment and this time I will not have to take any time out to recover from the ravages of the toxins, Chemotherapy and steroids. During the six months of Chemotherapy I did not attend the doctor once for infections even though I had attended the hospital, my blood counts were excellent.

What is most interesting and gratifying is that 5 weeks after my last treatment of Chemotherapy I played 9 holes of golf and I was back walking again. The last time I was on Chemotherapy it took 18 months to resume these activities. This time I had expected not to be able to do either of these until at least nine months after my last treatment. I am so surprised and delighted to be back doing my normal activities again.

The only thing different between the two treatments of chemotherapy is that I have been using the machines 4-6 times weekly. It is quite remarkable the difference these machines have made to me to the quality of my life during the latter part of the chemotherapy treatment and to my lifestyle on completing the course of chemotherapy.

I will continue to use the machines and later in the year buy them for home use. It is absolutely the difference they have made to my life.

Rena Condrot

Mercury Poisoning
Lance O'Brien

My husband had become very ill in 2009.

At first, he was presenting small pressure urticaria and swellings, but during our holiday to Romania, in October that year he developed severe lip, angioedema, face swelling and even internal swelling, being at high risk of anaphylactic shock. His blood pressure went extremely high as well, so I had brought him into ER in Coltea Hospital in Bucharest. The Doctor on duty ran blood tests, ECG heart test, Lung Scan and everything she could think off, but nothing seemed to come up in the tests.

She gave him an adrenaline shot and prescribed a course of Antibiotics, saying that the white cell count was indicating the presence of an infection which she thought was just a viral cold (nothing to do with the hives and swellings), but just to be sure she prescribed antibiotics. She gave him diuretics to keep the blood pressure under control. She said he should undergo further testing to find the cause of the swellings and urticaria and she mentioned LUPUS as a possibility...

We went back home. Lance was very week and pale at this time and tried to eat just very plain basic food, no preservatives, no pork (we had noticed that pork would be sometimes bringing urticaria flare up).

The next day, I brought him into the Laboratory of Cantacusino Institute in Bucharest to get more extensive blood testing done. The results were emailed to us after, nothing came up as abnormal in these tests and LUPUS was crossed out of the list of possible diagnosis.

We managed to fly back to Ireland and Lance was just very pale and getting weaker by the day and could get flares of urticaria and angioedema for no reasons. I remember one day he blew into a trumpet and his lips swelled so much - you would think he had silicone implants; it is funny now thinking back, but at the time was very scary.

We went to our GP and tried to get to the bottom of the problem. Lance was prescribed antiallergy tablets and stronger blood pressure tablets, but his condition didn't seem to improve…

He went to allergy tests in Charlemont Clinic in Dublin with no results.
He went to numerous consultations/ treatments with a dermatologist.

He went for consultations in Blackrock Clinic in Dublin only to be told to do a number of tests-Tests that Lance already had done in Romania.

He said he didn't want to go through the same tests again – we already knew the results – or better said – NO RESULTS. He just didn't have the strength to go through it all again…

At that time, it seemed that I just had to get used to the idea of losing him and I thought that my 2 small children ages four and three at the time, would probably have to face growing up without a father…

I just didn't want to give up. I sent desperate messages to my friends and family not knowing what to do. Neither Lance or I believed in magic healers or anything in this line...

The chairperson of the Motorcaravan Club of Ireland, whom we had dealings with through the nature of our business, recommended Agnes McGuinness. "She will tell you what is wrong with him", he said.

We were not convinced of that, but he didn't have much of a choice, we had to try everything or anything…

Lance went to her on December the 8th 2009 and she tested him for around 3 hours. She was able to tell him all that was wrong with him, blood poisoning by mercury in his teeth seemed to be the main problem.

It was a long way to recovery, but "you have to do what you are told" Agnes said, and things improved bit by bit.

- Following a strict detox
- Taking the supplements
- Removing the mercury fillings one by one (after each filling removal, Lance would get a bad flare of hives and swellings)
- Watching his diet
- Using bio-resonator treatment
- Getting tapped regularly…

It wasn't easy, but Lance is still with us now, no more hives and swellings, one more child in the family since, and it's all thanks to Agnes McGuinness.

Thank you, Agnes.

Vicky O'Brien, Co Kilkenny

Recovery after Surgery
Liam Crofton (62)

In March 2012 I was recovering after a lung operation which I had in 2009. I had been attending doctors and taking medications all those years but I was getting progressively sicker and I knew something was terribly wrong.

A good friend of mine (B) told me that he was worried about me and that I needed to see someone who could fix me. He made an appointment for me with a lady called Agnes McGuinness, I was willing to try anything at this stage as I was going downhill steadily.

On my first visit to Agnes I was surprised at the homeliness and her down to earth approach and I felt strait away that I was in the right hands.
Agnes tested me and then set out a treatment program, which I found hard at first, but manageable. I started that every day and after approximately three weeks I started to feel a change and I improved dramatically over the next couple of months.

I think I spent about six months on this programme, this was no hardship as I could see the improvement every day.
I owe my good health and wellbeing to Agnes and now not only see her as my saviour, I also consider her my "Granny ", also a good friend to both myself and my wife Mary, whom Agnes has also treated for various complaints.

God bless her.

Liam Crofton

Knee Injury

Johnny Lupton

On 17th November 1995, I had a bad fall on a small Japanese type bridge located in my garden. The weather was very cold (minus 4 degrees). My left leg was jammed under me at a an angle and caused the main muscle tendon on the patella to snap. Friends brought me to the Lourdes Hospital in Drogheda, the same night.

Following major surgery in the hospital during which, bore holes were made in the patella to draw threaded fibres through the patella to support re-attachment of the tendon. The operation as such was successful but a train of events was to follow which left me partially incapacitated for more than two years.

During the operation in Drogheda, a broken steel bit was left in my knee. While this piece is tiny, the Surgeon took the view that to try and remove it would cause too much damage to the bone. I was advised that the metal would not cause any problems in the future.

Some seven weeks later, the cast covering the damaged leg was removed to reveal a knee wound, which was leaking blood and showed a small disk area suggesting infection in the knee. One of the surgeons at the hospital decided to cauterise the infected area. This was to have a dramatic and long lasting response.

Several days later, physiotherapy commenced in order to create movement in the leg which had become stiff and very sore, and permitted very limited bending of the leg. After the first session, it was noticed that the area around the wound stitching was bleeding badly and some puss was apparent. It was decided by the Surgeon that I should re-enter the hospital for intravenous antibiotic treatment as the standard method of taking the antibiotics tablets orally had failed to defeat the infection. After twelve days on this programme, I was sent home to re-commence physiotherapy. Again, following initial exercise, the bleeding and infection returned. I was taken into the hospital again for further anti-biotic treatment. This was now in or about the month of March 1996.
The alarm bells were ringing and I insisted on a referral to another Surgeon at Beaumont Hospital in Dublin.

I was examined in Beaumont and a decision was taken to bring me into hospital for a further operation to re-open the knee and see what was going on. A programme, which involved exercising the wound on the knee, began in July 1996, during which it was discovered that the original sutures used in the Lourdes Hospital had become badly infected.

In June 1996 I met Agnes McGuinness during a social event in Gowran, Co Kilkenny. Her husband, Paddy had received a minor head injury and as a qualified First Aid person, I was asked to assist him. Agnes noticed the condition of my knee and she knew immediately that I was in serious trouble. She offered to help me. I graciously accepted this offer and attended her home in Clonalvy, Co Meath for a further detailed examination.

I briefed Agnes on the chain of events and told her that Beaumont Hospital wished to "clean out the wounded area". She advised me that this operation was vital. She told me that all aspects of the healing process have their place. Agnes could detect serious infection in my leg and told me, "this will never heal without proper treatment". I went into Beaumont and a programme of operations began. There were four separate operations to the knee area and the wound was kept open for approximately six weeks so that it could be cleaned every day. I was placed on a powerful dose of antibiotics, which drained my immune system and reduced my defence capability.

I should mention that the resident Microbiologist at Beaumont hospital had identified the infection in my leg as MRSA. Following initial treatment, the Surgeon became somewhat perplexed, as the wound was clearly not healing.

Agnes McGuinness began proper treatment of my leg in September 1996. She implied that I had to make a major decision and that was to "go off" the anti-biotic treatment from the Hospital, as it was obviously not working. She also placed me on a poultice using "Sheeps Sorrel Leaf" (found in fields and gardens) to draw the poison from the leg. Agnes was convinced that the hospital had not succeeded in cleaning all the infected material out of the knee area. The sorrel leaf was very effective in pulling out much of the infected tissue.

As I was still attending the hospital, the Surgeon was intrigued by the sorrel leaf and recorded its capability for hospital use. He admitted to me that the antibiotics were not working and if it was his decision for himself, "he would stay with Agnes in order to ensure an effective cure". This greatly surprised me as the medical profession generally tended to frown on complementary medicine techniques at that time. I went off the antibiotic treatment and Agnes began to step up her dedicated treatment campaign.

Agnes advised me that the whole chain of events from the time of the accident had reduced my immune defence capability to a very low ebb and left me in no doubt that I would have lost the leg (at the very least) if I had continued with the hospital treatment. This fact was later confirmed to me by an eminent surgeon.

Her first task was to change my bad eating habits and to make me aware of my environment. She said that my house was seriously contaminated by geopathic stress and it needed to be addressed immediately as the conditions there were interfering with the healing process. Jim Burke, a retired engineer carried out a dowsing investigation of my property and confirmed Agnes's statements to me. By placing anti-stress bars throughout the property, it eliminated any further dangers.

Point of Note

Every year (sometimes twice a year) I suffered from bronchitis. Following the treatment of my home by Jim Burke, this illness returned only once more than ten years ago. I can further state that I have not had as much as a head cold for several years. If I do feel the occasional "depression" it rarely lasts no more than a day. In addition to the installation of the anti-stress bars, I also attribute this to my re-education of proper eating and rest habits as taught to me by Agnes.

Agnes "adopted" me over the following two years from 1996. Her dedication to treating me to defeat this most virulent of infections resulted in a remarkable, consistent friendship which has stood the test of time. To say that I believe in her great ability to help and cure patients is an understatement and I have loyally sent many clients for her attentive care over the years (how she copes with everyone is a miracle in itself).

Agnes made me aware of the power of colour and steered me away from wearing dark colours all the time (even my underwear was lighter in colour). She showed me how colours around the home lift the spirit and how a peaceful atmosphere is very conducive to aiding recovery from any illness. She educated me to how the body truly reacts to proper attention and how the balance of my health lay within my own grasp on an on-going basis. Agnes has never refused my requests for advice or assistance for myself and for others.

The methods employed by Agnes McGuinness when treating people are a tribute to her remarkable talent and knowledge, not only of the human body and condition but the countryside and its great infusion of healing plants and flowers. She has dedicated her life to helping others and through her own capacity and great heart, I can attest to the results of her magnificent endeavour.

I have sat beside patients of hers, who would not have survived without her expert intervention. She is praised and loved by everyone who knows her and if people have not been cured, it says more about their own failings to adhere to good advice and attention, than to Agnes's wonderful treatments and renowned healing capability.

After nearly two years of battle, Agnes overcame my killer illness. The MRSA was destroyed. She improved my health to its highest level during this period.

My immune system was so powerful, I think it was strong enough to cure people standing beside me in bus queues. This may be an exaggeration but it indicates how I felt at the time.

Agnes saved my leg and my life. She was correct in her assessment that the leg still carried infection after five operations in two hospitals. In July 1997, a final badly infected suture was pushed out of my leg by my increasingly improved immune system, which was restructured and strengthened by Agnes. I had been listed for a further operation in the hospital and they were stunned to see the suture come out of my leg in such a fashion. I should also mention that my late mother's belief in the power of prayer would have been a contributory factor. I suggest that my mother's prayers were directed to Agnes to achieve a positive result for me. This she did with flying colours.

Epilogue

Agnes McGuinness is living proof of how one should live with what nature provides. All of us have the capability within ourselves to improve our lives. All we really need is the interest and the guidance of learned people.

My experience has taught me to be more observant and attentive to the world about me. I hold a 10th Degree Grand Master's grade in the Martial Art of Jiu-Jitsu and my knowledge of martial arts is very extensive. I have learned and seen much through the violence and physical pain involved in many hours of training and enforced discipline and I expect that my history in this regard assisted me greatly in adhering to the direction and vital requirements insisted on by Agnes, for me to have an effective cure. Regardless of my own personal knowledge, I say that all of that doesn't hold a candle to the knowledge and compassion demonstrated by Agnes down all her days.

My life has been the better for meeting and getting to know Agnes McGuinness. She is my great friend. She has been a great friend to all who have benefited from her wonderful talent and knowledge. She has a wonderful companion in her daughter-in-law Lorna who has equally given her time and absolute commitment to assisting Agnes in her works and it would be my personal wish that Lorna will carry on with the wondrous works and good will created and cemented by Agnes in her many, many years of selfless service to, sometimes and often, suffering community.

God Bless Agnes. May she have many more years to offer to those who greatly need her unique gifts in a time of increasing un-certainty. I can say without fear of favour, that I would not be writing this history and tribute without her timely intervention and extraordinary kindness, for which I am forever grateful.

Johnny Lupton, Co Meath, 9th February 2007

Parasites and Mercury fillings
David T Chambers

My first meeting with Agnes was almost 20 years ago, as a customer when she bought health related product from me. Over the pursuing years, Agnes has given me much helpful advice regarding my health and continues to do so.

She diagnosed a problem with various parasites and recommended the appropriate herbal medicine and more important how to take it, this type of knowledge is very much lacking today especially with much confusing information available via the internet. I believe my parasite problem was from my time spent working in Zaire (now DRC) in the 1990's.

One day when visiting Agnes, she just looked at me and said, get your mercury filling removed, which I did and it made huge difference to my general health. I was also advised to have a Liver & Kidney detox which I continue to do twice a year.

I continue to visit Agnes for regular health checks and follow her advice on what vitamins/ minerals to take. Due to the help from Agnes over the years and living a healthy lifestyle I am in rude health as I approach my birthday 72 years' young. I am privileged to able to list Agnes as one of my best friends she is one of the most caring people I know and has genuine interest in the health of those who visit her.

David T Chambers

Parasites
Brian Neill

I started seeing Agnes after 25 years of suffering with compromised health. Over the years I had been seen by four different gastroenterologists with no diagnosis and no relief. My head had been slowly deteriorating and I was at a very low ebb. I knew I was in trouble and I was on the verge of total despair.

On my first early morning visit to Agnes, I was greeted with a cup of coffee and homemade fruit cake. While I was enjoying my breakfast, she proceeded to examine the soles of my feet. Without asking any questions she was able to tell me the root cause of my problems- parasites. This made perfect sense to me as my problems had started about a year after a trip to Indonesia where I had a bad bout of dysentery after drinking contaminated water. She warned me that it would take time to clear these and build myself back up.

Agnes has a small machine called a Zapper so I got a few treatments on that. She prescribed herbs also, clove, wormwood and black walnut to kill the parasites. The rebuilding herb was turmeric and she recommended a clove of garlic. There were also some food that I had to take out of the diet because they didn't suit me and also some that I should add to my diet. It was all for the better. Over the last year of seeing Agnes every month the transformation has been remarkable. Parasites are not a pleasant thing to have. Not only do they rob your body of essential minerals and nutrients but the by products are toxic to the body as a whole.

Under Agnes's care it took a determined effort to build up the body again. Agnes has been extremely generous in sharing her vast knowledge and care. As a result I now feel alive again and equipped to maintain optimum health.

Brian Neill, Co Wexford

Sickness Bug
Paul (7)

Paul was brought to me with a sickness bug. He was not able to keep any food down. I gave him an abdominal massage starting from the right side in clockwise rotations, I asked his mother to do the same three times daily. I mixed 4 drops of Tea tree oil, 2 drops of peppermint, 2 drops of fennel and 2 drops of orange into 30ml ground nut oil. I also gave him Bach Flower Remedies and a child's Echinacea for the Immune System and plenty of water to drink. He was eating within 24 hours with no more sickness or nausea.

Cerebral Palsy
Paul (11)

Poor vision, hearing acute, fits would last about 12 to 15 minutes, sweating, poor movement. He had to be tied to a push chair as he could not hold his head up. Responses very poor. Mother in her 20's. Paul was badly infected with parasites. He also had mineral deficiency.

I treated him for the parasites with homeopathy. I also gave him Potassium Phosphate and Magnesium drops. He was to take these three times daily. No night fits after one week of treatment. Eight weeks later all fits had stopped. Soon after he was able to let his mother know when his nappy is wet. He started making sounds and was able to hold his head. He was smiling.

I recommended a daily lymphatic drainage massage for his mother and lymph treatment and nutritional diet.

Coma
Barry Murphy

"In July 2005 when I had just turned 30, I had a very bad stroke and was taken by ambulance to Beaumont Hospital where I was given no hope of recovering. I was in intensive care for 12 days in a coma. When I came around in August I had no power at all in my left side and couldn't walk or talk. While I was in that coma Agnes came to see me. She spoke to me and my eyelids flickered. This was the first sign of life in me. She checked my tongue and said I would make a good recovery. My parents were delighted as at this stage they were clutching at straws and this was their only hope and encouragement. I was eventually sent home to my local hospital where I had some physio and in October I was home in a wheelchair and a walking aid to get around. I never used the wheelchair after that and just struggled every day on the walking aid. In January 2006, my mother brought me to Agnes and she started to work on me. Twice a week I went to her. She did healing massage and reflexology on me and soon I started to feel more energy and become suppler and started to walk better. After 2 years, I was walking unaided, speaking properly and back driving on my own. All thanks to Agnes' help and encouragement. She has been an inspiration to me and without her I know I would not have kept going or been so motivated to get better.

Thank you, Agnes."

Barry Murphy

ME
Young Woman (23)

This young woman had this condition called ME for 2 years. Unable to lift her head and insufficient energy to walk 20 yards. I treated her for 4 days a week for 3 weeks. Her energy recovered and soon after she was able to live a normal life. I found 3 different contributors to her condition;

- Viral Infection, Coxsackie.
- Mercury poisoning, from dental fillings.
- Geopathic Stress, sleeping on a split-level bed.

Treatment included, Reflexology, weekly for 3 weeks. Oxygen therapy to restore her energy. Oscillator to kill bacteria. Homeopathic Coxsackie to detox virus. Bowel cleanse. Kidney Liquescence, Nervous System treated. Nourishing light diet. Fresh air.

Due to weak state of client, the mercury treatment was deferred until her Immune System had recovered alongside reasonable energy levels.

Mercury Poisoning
Joanne McNamara

"On 28th August 1993, I collapsed at work and lost the power of my right hand and leg and my speech went. Luckily for me it all started to come back within 24 hours. The doctor at the hospital diagnosed me with 'severe migraine'. I didn't believe the diagnosis so my GP decided to refer me to a neurologist. In work, I was referred for a CT Scan and MRI Scan which showed a scattered 'ischaemic area' in my brain.

At that time the neurologist diagnosed me with Multiple Sclerosis and said that when I get the next attack they would do a lumber puncture to confirm diagnosis. He told me to enjoy life and not have any more children as I would be in a wheelchair in 10 years' time. At that time my only child was 1 ½ years old. I started researching right side weakness and M.S. I had read where a Professor, Jack Hevenson (dentist) was doing research on mercury toxicity and M.S. At the time, I contacted him but as he was in London, it took time to contact him.

In the meantime, I was given Agnes McGuinness' name and phone no. I came to visit Agnes in September of 1994. Then my life changed forever. Agnes diagnosed me with mercury toxicity and an allergic reaction to formaldehyde. I was advised to remove all my mercury fillings and reverse root canal I had done 2 years previously. (2 years prior to all this I had dental work done in Limerick – my dentist at the time replaced my mercury fillings!!)

I went to Dr. McCallum, a dentist in Kilkenny. I had all my fillings replaced and I went on my detox plan and diet from Agnes. Within 12 months I was a new woman.

I still went ahead with research from Prof. Jack Hevenson. He ordered blood tests for me and he prescribed they showed up toxic levels of mercury and formaldehyde in my system. Exactly what Agnes had told me 3 months earlier.

I followed my detox diet rigorously and took Agnes' advise. 4 years later I went on to have my second child and another child after that.

Twenty two (22) years down the line I am perfectly healthy with 3 children and not in a wheelchair. I never had lumber puncture to confirm my diagnosis as I never got another attack.

Joanne McNamara, 9 Mar 2016

Pain over the Pancreas
Male (40)

This man had this continuous pain over his pancreas. He was toxic when I tested him at which point he said he worked with Glue. A case of occupational toxicity. Other symptoms indicated; The Urinary System and Bladder were affected. Backward pressure on Kidney resulting in Kidney swelling which put pressure on Pancreas.

Treatment included a hot bath every evening, St John's Worth Oil rubbed on the bladder area after hot bath. Reflexology for Bladder. Acupuncture for pain relief.

Leg Injury
Paddy

In September 1997, my husband got his leg badly broken by a kick from a cow suffering from grass tetany. We brought him to Mullingar Hospital and later he was sent by ambulance to Tullamore Hospital. Here they set his leg and it was so badly broken they had to insert a steel rod or pin. He got on well and about eighteen months to two years later began to get pain in the leg. I brought him back to various doctors and then to the man who did the operation on his broken leg. He said that at this stage the bone would have grown round the pin that had been inserted in his leg but as a last resort they would operate and take out the pin as by that stage the pain was pretty severe.

In the meantime, I was going to Agnes and my husband came with me. We were sitting in Agnes's hallway when she came out of her treatment room and asked Paddy how he was. He told her about the pain in the leg and how they were going to operate to take out the pin. While he was telling her this she took his hand and put her fingers on his arm somewhere between the wrist and elbow, maybe a bit nearer to the elbow. She exerted a good bit of pressure on the spot on his arm and I could see him sitting up straighter on his seat as he felt the pressure more. After a short time, she took her hand off his arm and you could see him relaxing. Then she asked him how was the pain in his leg, he looked at her, stood up and flexed his leg and then he said 'it's gone', and it stayed gone for the rest of his life and he hadn't to go back to Tullamore for an operation, thanks to Agnes.

Paddy died suddenly in 2010 from a heart attack but he never forgot what Agnes did for him and the suffering she saved him.

Injury at Birth
Baby Jack

Our son Jack was born on the 2nd Oct 2013. He weighed 10lb 7oz.

I had a very complicated birth with Jack. Jack was so big for a natural delivery but labour progressed so quick I had to deliver him naturally.

When Jack was born, he had 4 broken ribs and broken collar bone. He was very swollen and bruised. His little ears were squashed. Jack swallowed some of the amniotic fluid during labour. The doctors had to resuscitate Jack as he was very distressed after labour and stopped breathing. He spent 48 hours in ICU.

When Jack was 48 hours old the hospital did a hearing test and the result I was told was that Jack was deaf.

I called to Agnes McGuinness after we got home from hospital. I told Agnes about all the trauma Jack had during delivery and about the hearing test.
Agnes told me to roll out Jack's ears as they were curled down. I also had to put drops into Jack's ears.

After many weeks, I had to bring Jack for a hearing test in Dublin when he was about 4 months old, to be told Jack has perfect hearing after weeks of being told Jack was deaf.

While all this was going on Jack took a reaction to the formula I was feeding him. We went back to Agnes to get Jack tested. I had to change Jack's formula and change his feeding bottles to glass bottles. Within 2-3 weeks Jack was a happy, healthy, sleeping baby.

Jack is 3 years old now and would hear the grass grow. He is a very happy little boy.

Agnes McGuinness is truly a miracle worker. We are so grateful and thankful for all she has done for our little boy."

Keira & Ian Hand

Ataxia
(Impaired fine motor skills)

In a letter from a doctor in the year 2003, the doctor states, about our son, he has associated significant ataxia. He gets around the house with the aid of a walker and he will always need assistance with his daily activities. The daily activities will include dressing, feeding, toilet, etc.

In those early years, we were introduced to Agnes McGuinness who said from the beginning our son will be fine but you must put a lot of work into him. Agnes also said it was injections and our son needed these injections (national scheme of injecting babies). We were determined to try anything.

I did not understand alternative medicine and I was very cautious at the beginning. I have witnessed people make full recoveries from these ailments, which was amazing to see. Also, I know our son rarely visits hospitals. He is walking he is able to dress/undress himself, he is able to feed himself (also cooks), he is able to use toilet facilities by himself. He is able to get in and out of bath and wash himself. He is able to complete flips and back flips three times in a row in a swimming pool. I cannot even do that. He is able to drive his own small car. He can drive a small mini digger and a standard electric (2000 kg) fork lift and much more.

My wife has also put fantastic work into our son. Assistants, doctors teachers, clinics, etc. have also put great work into our son.

I know our son would not have come on so well without Agnes McGuinness and Lorna McGuinness and alternative medicine. They also have put incredible work into our son.

Go Raibh Maith Agaibh

September 2012

Infertility and other health issues
Adrian Redican

Geraldine and I got married in 2001 and for the next two years we tried very hard to have a baby, but to no avail. We had various tests and procedures done however, they failed to work. Geraldine was now 39 & time was not on our side. We heard about IVF treatment & attended a meeting, only to be told that Geraldine's chances of pregnancy was less than 15% which was devastating news for us.

We met Agnes & her late husband Paddy in Lourdes a few years earlier. It all started off by Agnes staring into my eyes one day while we were having lunch & she told me I was suffering severe pain from my sciatic nerve, I was gobsmacked, & it took off from there. Geraldine told Agnes about the IVF treatment & also her 15% chance of becoming pregnant. Agnes strongly advised Geraldine to go for the IVF treatment which she did. Agnes looked for a photo & DNA, a short piece of Geraldine's hair. Six weeks later Geraldine was pregnant carrying twins .

Bowel

I was passing small amounts of blood & looked for a colonoscopy to be done. A short while later the appointment came in the post. I phoned Agnes letting her know what I was doing because it had gotten worse & I feared the worst. Agnes assured me there was nothing there & to carry two small horse chestnuts in my pockets at all times. This will prevent pile's from forming. I did go to have the colonoscopy, and yes Agnes was right, nothing found.

Steel particle

I got a small steel fragment in my eye & I tried everything to wash it out but failed. I attended casualty and was left waiting for 5 -6 hours. I eventually contacted Agnes to see could she do anything, her answer was, "it will be out in 20 minutes." Sure enough it slowly came out. Just then the Doctor arrived & checked my eye. The Doctor could find nothing.

Headache

Often phoned Agnes about a headache, her cure was to comb my hair backwards using a steel comb. It always worked for me. She said there was too much electricity in my body.

Adrian Redican
Co. Mayo

Childhood Allergy
Ian Cunningham

History: Normal delivery, Weight 8lbs 11oz, had 3:1 injection. P.K.U. (normal) BCG at 5 days

Feb 1990 at 17 months: Abdomen became distended and this put pressure on the breathing and circulation as his lips were blue in colour. Brought to see Dr Yelverton and was sent straight to Lourdes Hospital. He had a chest X-ray, straight abdomen X-ray and had an ultrasonic scan. These showed up extensive build-up of wind in the colon. He was put on a drip to rest the bowel. Blood tests were normal, heart and lungs normal. It was suggested Ian had had food poisoning resulting in a build-up of wind. Before his admission to hospital he had vomited twice, had two runny nappies and was off food for a few days, but he had just cut 6 teeth at once.

No treatment was given in hospital. He was observed for 8 days. For the 2 days before he went home he got a head cold, had a little cough and was put on a nebulizer 4 times a day.

We got a second opinion in Crumlin Hospital with a Professor Guiney. He backed up what we were told in the Lourdes. I got sulphur tablets for Ian and this seemed to give ease. Slowly the abdomen returned to normal. Professor Guiney also suggested that Ian might have a food allergy.

Jun 1990: Ian started snoring at night. He also started having difficulty swallowing some solid foods. I often had to remove food from the back of his throat. The G.P. referred him to Dr McCullen (E.N.T. Surgeon). Enlarged Tonsils and Adenoids were diagnosed and he was admitted to Lourdes at 21 months to have both tonsils and adenoid removed. This went well and Ian was automatically put on routine antibiotic following surgery.

Aug 1990: We noticed Ian getting short of breath. If he ran a little he would end up coughing and looking for breath. Afterwards he would have these little coughs which were irritating and he had these throughout the day. Then the wheeziness came, at first it was bubbly wheeze and became more severe. He was distressed with it. I brought him to the G.P. Dr. Yelverton. He could hear the wheeze and listened to the lungs where some noises were heard. Ian was prescribed an antibiotic and told to come back in 1 week. There was no improvement. The coughing would start after Ian went to bed. He would get a little sleep and at 5 or 6 in the morning the cough would start and could last for several hours. He continued to be wheezy on exertion. Back to the G.P. after 1 week. Ian was put on a stronger antibiotic.

I asked about a second opinion and Dr. Yelverton said he would make an appointment with Dr. Murphy (Paediatrition in Lourdes). I stopped the second antibiotic because I felt it was not helping. In the meantime, one morning when I gave Calpol to one of the other children, Ian took some of the Calpol himself. I wasn't sure how much he had taken so to be on the safe side I took him to the hospital. He was given 'Epicac' to make him sick, which worked. He had bloods taken to see if there were any traces of it in his system. Because of his chest problem I asked if he could be admitted and hopefully be seen by the Paediatrition. He was admitted (Saturday), observed and seen by Dr. Murphy on the Monday. She examined him, got him exercising and noted his wheeze and cough. She agreed he was Asthmatic, and discharged him on Slowphyllin tablets. (1 at night and 1 in the morning). If this did not control the wheeze she said, he would have to be put on an inhaler. He was given an appointment to see Dr. Murphy in 6 weeks.

Need another opinion

After 2 weeks on the tablets we were not happy. John wanted Ian to see Agnes McGuinness for testing. I stopped his tablets. I didn't want Ian to be asthmatic or be treated like one. I knew what a distressing illness it was.

When we brought Ian to see Agnes, he was coughing nearly every hour of the day. He had no energy and couldn't walk without wheezing. He was almost 3 years old. Agnes tested him. He was allergic to a lot of foods and especially to food additives, colours, flavours etc. Out went ice-cream, snax (crisps), chocolate, ice-pops, sausages, packet soup, vinegar, cheese, cereals (except porridge), peanuts, potatoes, sweets, flour. I was not to put powder on him. I was shown how to massage his back and chest, how to work on his feet. Agnes also recommended stem and eucalyptus to loosen the cough. Ginger also helped to loosen the cough. He was put on homeopathic tablets and drops for his cough and also on a worm dose, as he had worms present.

Agnes also showed me how to do a full body drainage system on him and this was done daily. On every visit Ian would also have Magnet Therapy. We visited Agnes regularly over the first couple of weeks. The wheeze went within the first 2 weeks and the cough got looser and less frequent. Agnes advised us to move Ian's bed as it was in a stress line. This we did. We also replaced feather pillows and blankets for a duvet. Ian was put on drops for Geopathic Stress. Ian began to get a full night's sleep. I followed Agnes's instructions every day. When Ian went back to see Dr Murphy in the hospital, I didn't say I had stopped the tablets or was attending anyone else. I didn't want any arguments. Dr Murphy listened to Ian's chest and examined him and agreed that his chest was perfect.

I was told there would be no need for an inhaler, and to continue with Ian's tablets for another year, as they seemed to be working well. I could try him without the tablets then to see if it made any difference, and if there were any problems to make another appointment. I never returned.

Ian is also on goat's milk, which I have never given up. He was gradually able to go back on a lot of the foods but he does not have any artificial additives or colours or flavours. He can have treats from time to time. For the first couple of years after seeing Agnes he would occasionally get croup, for which he would have foot massage, magnet therapy and steam inhalation and eucalyptus. We were always able to treat him without the use of antibiotics or tablets. He has not had antibiotics since we discovered natural cures. He hasn't even had a cough in the last few years. He enjoys swimming, running, football and Irish Dancing. When he was 8 he beat a few 12 year olds in two races and wasn't out of breath. Changing Ian's way of eating, and all the work that had to be done on him which seemed hard at the time, but it was a gradual process and well worth all the effort, when I see how healthy he is now.

Ian Cunningham, Co. Louth

Depression

In 2013 my son was under a lot of pressure from work and was looking forward to his holidays. He went to the states with his friend but after a day or so he felt really bad and decided to come home.

He was very weepy and upset and this continued for some time. I told Agnes about him and he went up to her for treatment. He was feeling really bad and as he had been with my other son when they discovered their father dead, he needed attention. Agnes gave him medication and he went two to three times per week for massage, tapping and to do the machines. Agnes looked after him very well, she listened to him, talked to him and understood the way he was feeling and then treated him as was needed.

This went on for over a year as he was very depressed, but thanks to Agnes he is in great health now both mentally and physically.

Anna Cassidy

Thrush (Candida)

Trina Cunningham

In 1990 I began to feel very tired. I could sleep for 13 hours and not feel rested. In the morning after a long sleep I could not get out of bed. My husband would get the 3 children up feed and clothe them then help me out of bed. It would take me an hour to start moving properly. It was put down to caring for my father who had passed that year and I had spent long hours looking after him.

During the day, I would eat full meals and craved sweet things and would eat up to 4 bars of chocolate. My weight was slowly going down. I started to feel pains in the fingers and toes. This was constant. Another trip to the doctor? Arthritis – Rheumatoid? The test was negative for that. I was put on arthritic and anti-inflammatory tablets.

Next my foot got inflamed and my ankle was red and swollen. I was given antibiotics for this. It eventually subsided. The next symptoms I had was sitting up in bed at night and belching up wind. Shortly after this I had palpations. Another visit to the doctor and the conclusion was, I was stressed. The doctor for the second time ordered bloods for a full blood count to see if I was anaemic. All results came back good. I had a chest X-ray and a thyroid function test done but all were inconclusive.

The next thing to happen was I got diarrhoea and didn't know what the cause was. It was severe and I lost a further half stone in weight. I had a specimen diarrhoea sent for testing. I was referred for a colonoscopy and a surgical opinion. All was done and again came back inconclusive. By this time the diarrhoea had stopped and the surgical doctor suggested I might be bulimic. I stressed to him I wasn't bulimic, as I have never vomited and had eaten well and never took laxatives.

Then I went to see Agnes McGuinness for testing. Within 2 minutes she told me I had thrush (Candida) and that it had gone right through the heart area and bowel.

I was put off sugar and yeast and had to take Acidophilus and Miso and various other dietary supplements. Within 4 days the pain in the fingers and toes went. From about 2 weeks later I began to get my energy back. Six weeks later I was tested again and allowed to go back on yeast and sugar gradually. I stuck rigidly to all Agnes's instructions and maintained my well-being and to this day see her regularly for reflexology. I have never looked back. Thank you Agnes.

Trina Cunningham, Co Louth

My personal experience of working with Agnes Mc Guinness from 1984 to the present day

Sr Helen McKenna

I first met Agnes Mc Guinness in 1987. We were both at one of Fr F Fox's week-long seminars in Newry. I had come home from Tanzania for my home leave. I had been introduced to Reflexology and out of necessity I was using it to supplement the one month's supply of donated essential Medicines. There was never enough medicine to treat everyone so I found a Reflexology book and realised I could help the patients with pain relief, among other things. I had planned to take a course in Reflexology but it was not easily available at that time. But I was assured that I 'would like Fr Fox'. Agnes by this time was well experienced in the ways of Natural Medicine.

During this course, Agnes offered to 'do my feet' (Reflexology) and oh, did it hurt! To be fair to her, I was taking my second course of antibiotics in as many weeks. After my first experience of Agnes's Reflexology, I refused to take off my shoes for the remainder of the week! As time went on I quickly learned that there was healing in Agnes's touch even if it hurt a little at the time. During each home leave from Tanzania, I found my way to Agnes's home and Treatment Rooms.

Agnes is one of the few 'true followers' of Fr Fox's extraordinary healing system – Bio-testing and Homeopathy. His protocol allows one to test the client for 'toxins' and find in which organs of the body they have got lodged. The second part of the protocol is to use the Homeopathy remedies and Tissue Salts to detox/ remove the offending toxins from the body. This process is so gentle and non-invasive and yet incredibly effective. This is the work that Agnes has perfected over the past 45 years. Agnes has never stopped learning and is always eager to expand her knowledge. Her treatment room wall, literally covered with Certificates, is a witness to her varied and broad background within the Natural Therapy field. During 2004 and 2006, I was fortunate to be based in Drogheda. I travelled out to Clonalvy once a week and to be mentored by Agnes as she treated her clients. While Agnes used a form of Kinesiology to test her clients, I firmly believe Agnes already knew what the client's problem was, even without testing.

Thanks to Agnes's encouragement, I now have my own Treatment Rooms in Arusha, Tanzania. Here I treat mostly the local neighbours as well as anyone who has got to hear about me.

It is such a joy to see people who have spent a fortune on medicines whose only function is 'symptom suppression', learn that there is another way – that of Bio-testing and Homeopathy, taught by Fr Fox back in England and Ireland. Being the generous woman that she is, Agnes is always ready to share her knowledge with others. This has led Agnes to give many seminars of her own over many years. My regret is that much of this material was not recorded in any form so it is a great joy to know that at last, Agnes's work will be reproduced on paper.

Sr Helen Mc Kenna
Medical Missionaries of Mary
1st February 2017
Feast of St Brigid

References

1. **Kinesiology** - The diagnostic tool to identify information and messages from the sub-conscious - Angela Burr Madsen. Positive Health Online, Issue 219, Dec 2014.

2. **Silent Spring** - Dr Rachel Carson. Houghton Mifflin Company. ISBN 0-618-24906-0.

3. **Tired or Toxic** - Dr Sherry Rodgers MD. Prestige Publishing. ISBN 0-9618821-2-

4. **Heavy Metals and Human Health** - Arif Tasleem Jan 1,*,†, Mudsser Azam 2,†, Kehkashan Siddiqui 2, Arif Ali 2, Inho Choi 1,* and Qazi Mohd. Rizwanul Haq

5. **Dental Mercury Toxicity and Bio-Regulatory Medicine** – Dr Stephen Bourne

6. **Obesity, a modern, mismanaged, and misunderstood malady** - Dr Heli Goode. Positive Health Online, Issue 232, Aug 2106.

7. **The Cure for all Cancers** - Dr Hulda Clark PhD ND. New Century Press. ISBN 1-890035-00-9.

8. **The Prevention of all Cancers** - Dr Hulda Clark PhD ND. New Century Press. ISBN 1-890035-34-3.

9. **Cancer and Homeopathy** - Dr Jean-Lionel Bagot. Unimedica, Narayana Verlang, Nlumenplatz 2, D-79400, Kandern, Germany.

10. **Cancer, Cause and Cure** - Percy Weston. Bookbin Publishing. ISBN 0-9758137-0-6

11. **The Hidden Drug - Dietary Phosphate** - Herta Hafer. Georg Thieme Verlag. ISBN 0-646406-44-2

12. **Healthy Aging, You are what you eat, drink, sleep exercise and practice.** www.nhacademy.eu

13. **The pH Balance** - Dr Robert O Young and Shelly Young. Piatkus Books UK. ISBN 9 780749 939816.

14. **Heal Your Body** - Louise Hay. Hay UK, Astley House, 33 Notting Hill Gate, London W11 3JQ

15. **Porphiria. The Ultimate Cause of Chronic Disease** - Stephen Rochlitz, PhD. ISBN 978-0-945262-59-6

16. **Gut and Psychology Syndrome** - Dr Natasha Cambell Mc Bride. Maidnform Publishing. ISBN 0-99548520-2-8

17. **Medical Medium** - Anthony William. Hay House. ISBN 978-1-78180-536-7

C

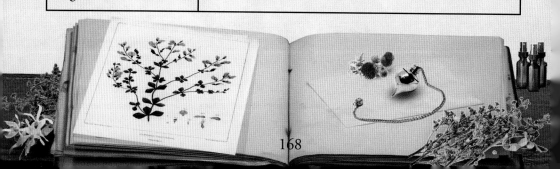

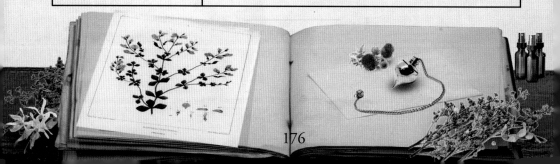